Universal Principles of Branding

Mark Kingsley

100 Key Concepts for Defining, Building and Delivering Brands

Quarto.com

© 2023 Quarto Publishing Group USA Inc.
Text © 2023 Mark Kingsley
Photography and illustrations © 2023 Mark Kingsley

First published in 2023 by Rockport Publishers, an imprint of The Quarto Group,
100 Cummings Center, Suite 265-D, Beverly, MA 01915, USA.
T (978) 282-9590 F (978) 283-2742

Rockport Publishers titles are also available at discount for retail, wholesale, promotional, and bulk purchase. For details, contact the Special Sales Manager by email at specialsales@quarto.com or by mail at The Quarto Group, Attn: Special Sales Manager, 100 Cummings Center, Suite 265-D, Beverly, MA 01915, USA.

10 9 8 7 6 5 4 3 2 1

ISBN: 978-0-7603-7820-5

Digital edition published in 2023
eISBN: 978-0-7603-7821-2

Library of Congress Cataloging-in-Publication Data

Names: Kingsley, Mark (Creative director), author.
Title: Universal principles of branding : 100 key concepts for defining,
   building, and delivering brands / Mark Kingsley
Description: Beverly, MA : Rockport Publishers, 2023. | Series: Rockport
   universal | Includes index. | Summary: "Universal Principles of Branding
   is a concise, visual introduction to 100 of the most fundamental
   elements of branding"-- Provided by publisher.
Identifiers: LCCN 2023018479 | ISBN 9780760378205 (hardcover) | ISBN
   9780760378212 (ebook)
Subjects: LCSH: Branding (Marketing) | New products. | Brand name products.
   | Advertising--Management.
Classification: LCC HF5415.1255 .K57 2023 | DDC 658.8/27--dc23/eng/20230530
LC record available at https://lccn.loc.gov/2023018479

Design: Mark Kingsley
Page Layout: Sporto

Printed in China

For you, my colleague.

CONTENTS / ALPHABETICAL

CONTENTS / CATEGORICAL

Delivering a Brand

INTRODUCTION

It seems contradictory to begin a collection of universal concepts by attacking the very idea of universality. But the reality is that one-size-fits-all thinking runs counter to the rich diversity found in contemporary branding. Unfortunately, practitioners tend to apply their own collection of strongly held framing devices to this increasingly complex profession. And they do it so dogmatically that their "professionalism" turns them into snobs. That profoundly limits them.

One "universal" concept that seems to be the cause of so much trouble in the world today is the idea of essentialism. In such a view, there are attributes that imbue things with authenticity. Attributes that make them, essentially the thing in discussion. For example, only the Champagne region can produce champagne, while the rest of the world merely produces sparkling wine, even if they follow the traditional champagne production method. And only the Kimberly-Clark corporation can produce Kleenex, while every other company produces facial tissue. Very quickly the value propositions and protectionism of essentialist thinking present themselves. This sense of authenticity, integral to prevailing approaches to branding, is worth money.

While branding professionals tend to frame things in an essentialist manner, that is not necessarily how brands behave in the minds of their audiences. As the branding and consumer research pioneer Walter Landor famously said

"PRODUCTS ARE MADE IN THE FACTORY, BUT BRANDS ARE CREATED IN THE MIND."

This means brands are basically interpretive acts.

If we take a lesson from current views of gender as a flexible, free-floating definition not caused by other stable factors like anatomy, then perhaps brands are equally decoupled from their associated objects. A producer, service provider, or organization may present an offering, but it requires an audience to complete the brand—thus establishing the respective expectations of behavior, value, and attraction.

This decoupling has a profound effect on the power dynamics of brands and branding. Commonly heard phrases within agencies, like "building the brand" or "bringing the brand to life," now seem arrogant, if not slightly deluded. The metaphoric method of brand dissemination shifts from a few centralized channels hammering in the same message (as it was during the Mad Men era) to a radar array receiving signals from numerous sources. Our own personal identities are the result of a negotiation of inputs, evaluated against a variety of received standards. We are prisms of multitudes.

The principles presented here were articulated with this in mind. To hold strict essentialist ideals when discussing one of the most interdisciplinary fields of contemporary life is to ignore the multitude of voices, needs, and experiences present in an increasingly complex world.

We all have much to learn. And as soon as we see without preconceptions, with an ear open to things as spoken, then thinking can prosper. The hope is that this work will play a small role in reframing branding as the cultural and aesthetic arrangement that emerged while markets were otherwise focused on returns.

Hopes for this book

Anyone working in today's marketplace works in branding—to some degree. And anyone living in modern society is equally affected by branding.

Too much material on the creation, dissemination, and maintenance of a brand tends to create, or expect, a passive audience. A methodology is devised, then presented with the intention that if a reader follows each step, they too will create a perfect brand. This seems inappropriate for the messiness of the world and how brands circulate in that world. Rather it is the goal for these principles to spark dialogue, reflection, and empathy instead of being seen as a recipe for the ideal brand. See them as entry points or moments to reflect.

While the selected principles attempt to cover the history of a brand—from definition to creation to delivery—across the spectrum of brand touchpoints— from the visual to the sonic to the environmental—the hope is that the cumulative effect will convey a sense of permission, and perhaps a degree of liberation for all parties involved. This could be the acceptance of foreign ideas, the amateur, or the unexpected as brand aspects worthy of consideration. Use these principles as a checklist, but also use them as provocations and tools to reframe preconceptions.

One aspect of creativity is "allowing" things to come into being. Let's simply begin by saying "yes."

1 ABSTRACTION

A defining quality of human existence is a capacity for abstract thinking. Even the most unsophisticated of us compress complex ideas into understandable expressions. And brands allow us to do it with increasing ease and increasing levels of complexity.

Let's begin with the first great abstraction: language. It may have originated through onomatopoeia; through duplicating the sounds of animals and natural phenomena (Meow! Tweet tweet!); through bodily movement (Ugh! Erg!); as social interjections (Ow! Oh!); through play or other intimate behavior (Mmm…); as a way to maintain social contact (Hey!); or a combination of all of them.

As the earliest words were combined into rudimentary phrases, the ability for complex ideas developed from there. And gradually we went from "the antelope is grazing by the tree" to the higher abstraction of "the 80s called; they want their shoulder pads back."

Our abstractive abilities go far beyond words and language. Photographs and films are two-dimensional abstractions of a three-dimensional world. And when, or if, we fully enter the multiverse, we may experience abstractions of time, gravity, and being—perhaps even sitting down to a meeting on a space station across from a killer whale in a cowboy hat.

Brands, too, are high-level abstractions. An often-repeated phrase states that a brand is not a logo. This is correct. The whole visual identity system—logo, color palette, patterns, typographic standards, photographic criteria—compress complex ideas and values into a shorthand for how anyone interacting with the brand should feel.

Brands are more than abstractions of things or ideas. They are abstractions of ways of being, ways that may be full of internal contradictions but are absolutely authentic to themselves. Gwyneth Paltrow's Goop brand offers luxury garden hose kits, work gloves, men's cuff links, and candles that smell like her vagina. The only thing that connects them is a sense of "Gwyneth-ness." And that Gwyneth-ness is somehow perfectly coherent, perfectly Goopy.

Even consumer packaged goods (CPG) brands with questionable nutritional value, like Kellogg's Frosted Flakes can authentically promote healthy living with a tagline ("They're gr-r-reat!") and corporate initiatives that promote high school sports programs.

This is the power of branding: the abstracting ability of the human mind to discover ways of being through an orchestrated combination of product, marketing, emotions, and culture.

Kellogg's Frosted Flakes is an American brand which uses the
name Frosties in the UK, European Union, and Israel.

2 ANTHROPOLOGY / ETHNOGRAPHY

Reaching a human
audience requires human
observation.

In order to better serve and respond to their audience, brands need to understand how they fit into people's lives. And the awareness stemming from customer and market research has been fundamentally transformed with the application of big data. Never before have strategists been able to develop such accurate insights and targeting with such large amounts of rich data, all filtered through algorithms enhanced with machine learning.

But such data measures only past events. Even "real-time" tracking is historical. And in the aggregate, it is limited to the what, the how, and the common. What if one wants to tap into larger trends that are not yet fully articulated? What if one wants to examine any gaps in the data or understand the why? Then one begins an ethnographic analysis, which then contributes to an anthropological inquiry.

Ethnography is the localized, hands-on description of life as it is lived and experienced. Good ethnography is contextual, sensitive, richly detailed, and, most importantly, depicts conditions as they are without editorializing. It is a slow, deliberate process, which is why much ethnography done in the discovery phase of branding projects tends to be generalized and with little nuance.

One method of ethnographic research is participant observation, where one joins a group for data collection. The raw material of participant observation—notes, photographs, collected objects—is often very messy because it's compiled in the moment. This material is then organized into an ethnographic report from which an organic process of discovery develops.

That discovery can then be the work of trend forecasting; or it can be the basis of a larger inquiry into the conditions and possibilities of what it is to be human. The social theories resulting from that process are what is known as anthropology—or, in the world of branding, the strategic upfront.

It is also possible to view participant observation as an anthropological study in itself. In such a case, the anthropologist studies *with* people instead of bracketing them as *objects of study*. The difference comes from intention, and both are valuable. Studying with varieties of people is a great way to develop a sensitivity to the gaps and/or differences between cultures, which can then lead to better questions in future research. And it provides the intellectual means with which to speculate on the conditions of human existence. This also is the reason why well-traveled and experienced people tend to make better branding practitioners.

Good ethnography, anthropology, and branding all stem from a spirit of openness and generosity. The settings are along the lines of "how do you…," "why do you…," and "what if…" instead of "you should…," "you shouldn't…," and "this is how…." Each corresponds with its subjects instead of speaking for them, and each works on varying levels. And, when applied in a brand context, this mindset helps produce work that is meaningful, real, global, and inclusive.

The author's photo was taken in the Tsukiji fish market as part of an ethnographic research trip to Tokyo.

3 ASSOCIATION

Brands trigger our associative memory, not our historical memory.

If I tickle your nose with a feather, where is the tickle located?

We begin with simple perception: a color, a shape, a smell, a sound—mere stimuli entering our sensory system without any attachment or meaning whatsoever. It is only when we begin to attach associations, and language to those stimuli that they now become the color yellow, two arch-like shapes, the smell of meat, and the sound of a restaurant.

We live in a world of associations. Everything that we perceive is framed by language, even if it doesn't have a name. An unknown phenomenon becomes a new thing, a thing that looks like food, a thing that fits in my hand, a thing that smells delicious. And those associations are reflections of a particular moment in culture, our lived experience, and our personal use of language.

Our consciousness is always directed toward something. We decide whether to consider it. We figure out whether it's familiar or not. And we give it a description. Things don't self-order themselves into our consciousness. They don't declare themselves as chair, table, or dog. They just are. We do the spontaneous job of comparing the thing in front of us against all possibilities and then settling upon chair, table, or dog.

This means we know things in a negative capacity. Consider that for a moment. Logos do not represent a company immediately upon creation; rather, they become associated with a company with exposure over time. The color black, for example, was not declared the color of heavy metal music by official edict. It became associated with heavy metal because it also had a whole host of heavy metal-adjacent associations with "the dark arts," the clang of coal-fueled factories, the night, and so on.

Perhaps a brand is better thought of as a specific node in a network of associations. The previously listed color yellow, two arch-like shapes, the smell of meat, and the sound of a restaurant now cluster into the affiliation commonly known as McDonald's. Which then means that every other point within the associative network known as McDonald's has the potential to either build or erode how people perceive the brand.

All of this has an effect on what we should expect from brands, their creators, and their audiences. It now seems ridiculous for a designer to authoritatively present a visual identity by saying, "Here is your new logo." Or for a company's head to think they have the final determination in whether something is "on brand" or not. Because that brand "tickle" occurs in the mind of the audience—somewhat out of control.

The question "If I tickle your nose with a feather, where is the tickle located?" illustrates a fundamental concept of phenomenology.

4 AUTHENTICITY

A brand's authenticity
does not always stem
from a single product.

Around the ninth or tenth century, the term "damascus" appeared to describe a sword that was capable of being sharpened to a very sharp edge and could withstand continued battle without shattering. Such a weapon was made from ingots of wootz steel, imported from India, and had a distinctive, water-like pattern on its surface. This pattern became a visual cue to the weapon's quality, and, in effect, an early example of a brand's visual identity. A logo, for all intents and purposes.

Jump ahead a millennium to Apple's Macintosh: the first successful mass market personal computer with a graphical user interface and only 128 kilobytes of RAM. As subsequent models added more memory, faster chips, greater storage capacity, and better graphics; adjacencies began to appear. Printers, scanners, modems, and disc drives were some of the first peripherals to the basic computer line, followed by laptops, handhelds, and fancier monitors.

If the basic function of computers centers around digital files, then a whole other set of adjacencies appears: iPods, earbuds, and, eventually, the iPhone—with a sophisticated camera array. This ongoing process of more powerful computers supplanting previous models and peripheral devices expanding the capacity of the line is in effect a process of substitution. One device may be substituted for another, but the improvement of products establishes a lineage of authenticity. One that is confirmed with the Apple logo, much like how the pattern of Damascus steel confirmed a blade's quality.

But Apple's expanded product line opened up territories beyond computers and peripherals. The iPod needed a music store with the same ease of use as the Mac operating system: iTunes. And, like the Apple computer line, the iPhone needed a portfolio of third-party apps to make it useful: the App Store.

And because the iPhone is portable, and has the potential for financial transactions, the need arises to verify identity and establish trusted interactions, thus spawning the Apple ID and the Apple Card.

How does this all hang together as authentically Apple? A credit card is quite a distance from a personal computer. One cannot simply follow a line of substitutions with one physical object replacing another. Instead there is an abstract process at play: one of nomination. Because Apple has a tradition of ease-of-use and reliability, established by its hardware, the equally easy and reliable credit card can now be nominated into that sphere of authenticity.

Traditionally a brand's authenticity is built upon its values and behaviors. But given the increasing blurring and diffusion of brands across digital/physical spaces, cultural contexts, and class distinctions; the growing number of brand extensions and partnerships; and how the materiality of markets seems to be disappearing one can get a sense for how this nomination process further shifts the branding profession away from previously reliable processes of design, production, distribution to a more complicated series of proposals, collaborations with unrelated brands, temporary offerings, and experiments.

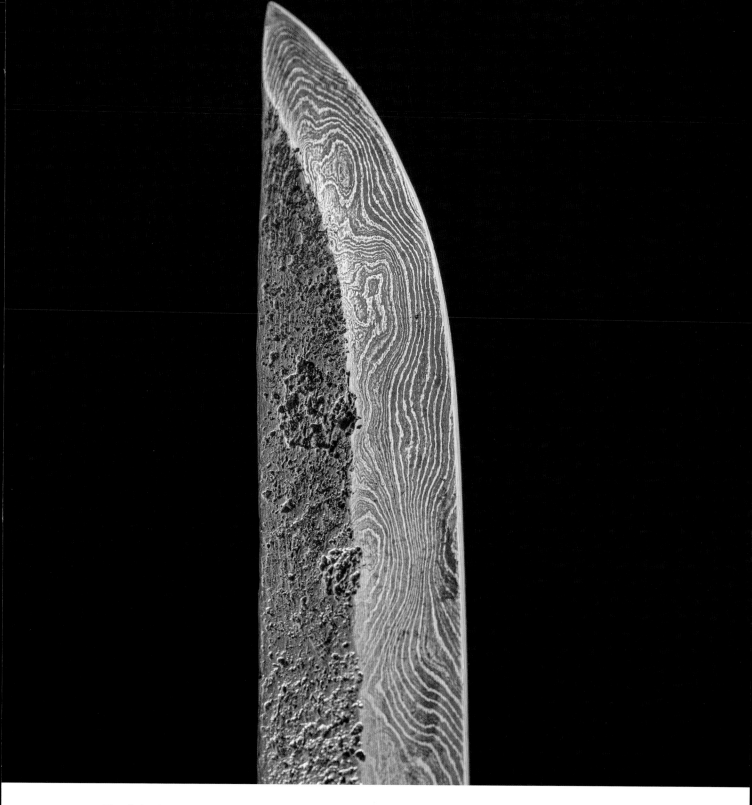

The distinctive pattern of Damascus steel is one of the earliest visual brand identities.

5 BANDITS AND ROBOTS

Every time you encounter a recommendation algorithm on Netflix, Google, Spotify, or Amazon, you run into a multiarmed bandit. Named after casino slot machines (known as "one-armed bandits"), they are algorithms designed to serve large, complex user bases with the goal of increasing customer engagement and revenue. Bandits filter user, product, and contextual metadata through methods relevant to the brand and then deliver personalized, dynamic content.

Whenever a static metric needs to be optimized, digital companies apply A/B testing. In that scenario, alternatives are swapped out randomly until a final winner is declared. The most famous A/B test occurred in 2009 when Marissa Mayer, then Google's vice president of search products and user experience, tested 41 shades of blue to find the color with the greatest click-through rate.

While the stages of A/B testing are static and distinct, multiarmed bandits adjust throughout all phases of the test. Each step generates information about the current state. This information, along with experience gathered from previous rounds, is used to determine an ideal subsequent action.

Bandit-based recommendation systems come in three general forms: collaborative filtering, which assumes that people who agreed in the past will agree in the future; content-based, which is built on aspects of the user-item relationship (gender, age, location, etc.); or a hybrid of the two. Given the success of brands currently enhancing their content delivery via recommendation algorithms, this seems to be working quite well.

But that model is geared toward the middle. As a user, once you arrive within a defined audience, that definition becomes more and more constrictive. If you respond favorably to recommendations, the more you will receive those recommendations. And in domains like streamed films or music, that begins to feel like a restrictive diet.

For example, twentieth-century pianists Thelonius Monk and Glenn Gould both had unorthodox performance styles and philosophical approaches to their specific genres: Monk in jazz and Gould in classical music. Both continue to have significant influence, decades after their passing. And even though Monk and Gould's music are different in sound, production, and performance, they shared a spirit of childlike wonder.

The only way to sense that connection would be to hear music from each in sequence; something that a recommendation algorithm probably isn't programmed to provide. In Spotify's case, the collaborative and content-based bandits skew toward popularity, and the potential for a deeper discovery is passed over in favor of an anodyne result.

Many times, it is easy to be dazzled by technological innovation and revenue. But when a brand's main offering is content and content recommendation, and the whole wondrous sense of discovery occurs at the edges of form and popularity, it seems that algorithmic bandits and robots pale in comparison to any recommendation (or provocation) coming from a thoughtful and informed human being.

Similar to a game of tic-tac-toe, multiarmed bandits adjust
throughout all phases of the test.

6 BEAUTY, NOT BEAUTIFICATION

A thoughtful consideration of beauty may offer surprising brand possibilities.

Beauty is not always the main goal for a brand, but its presence inescapably informs discussions on development and engagement. Pleasure and appeal are individual experiences that are difficult to describe. No single definition of aesthetic pleasure appears to be satisfactory. All, in some way, are inadequate both to pleasure in art and pleasure in nature. And since a main intention of brands is to evoke some aesthetic response, a broad discussion of beauty can be worthwhile.

A good start would be to remove taste from the discussion. Taste is too narrow a lens and frequently ends up separating people. Having "good taste" elevates some while diminishing others. A brand may appeal to a certain taste, but to focus only on that narrow audience is limiting. Taste restricts, and it constricts.

While taste has an ability to be defined, beauty, on the other hand, is purely without intellectual entanglement. It is an event, one that cannot be experienced at will nor be re-created. We encounter beauty, uncoerced.

Beauty moves between the joy of recognition and a melancholy of the passing moment. This movement underscores its ephemerality. Beauty is uninterested in any subject it might encounter; but an object may conform to allow for beauty. Flowers perceived as beautiful is the result of evolutionary adaptation on the part of the flower and the perceiver.

The ambiguity of beauty does not follow strategic positioning. This places it in tension with how brands are developed. A board of directors cannot create beauty, but it can beautify through style. Beautification is superficial, disconnected from fundamental uses and universal truths of existence. It reacts to time and history. When things become unfashionable or worn over time, the response is beautification.

Brands that offer stylistic approaches are not sustainable, either as a unique selling point, a consumable product, or in a material/environmental manner. There is an exhibit value to beautification and style. Style can be consumed, updated, and consumed again, while beauty cannot. Style is overdescribed, overfamiliar, and overconcretized, while beauty remains outside that cycle.

The challenge then for anyone working in branding is to step outside their ego and let beauty emerge. Even if it falls outside of existing brand guidelines, or if the audience takes things to an unexpected place, like the reinvention of blue jeans from symbol of hard work to rebellion to the office. That's OK. Beauty, the product of hospitality, acceptance, and lived experience, has greater connective potential than the transactional, insistent, and captioned world of style.

There is a reason why the great modernist designers all insisted that "less is more." They weren't speaking about detail but rather about the cognitive and economic demands of objects conforming to the newest fashions. For them, a world touched by beauty is far more appealing than a world festooned in style.

Top: Much of the beauty of architect Le Corbusier's Villa Savoye in Poissy near Paris, France, is seen in the way one moves through the building and how views are revealed.
Bottom: The banality of developments found across the United States comes from building styles that are overdescribed, overfamiliar, and overconcretized.

7 THE BIG FIVE

Five basic personality traits can offer insights into a brand's audience.

There are numerous approaches to analyzing a brand's audience. Currently one popular understanding of individual personality is the Big Five. First developed by American psychologist Donald W. Fiske in 1949, the Big Five was the result of years of attempts to easily understand the full dimensions of a person's behavior and character. Previous researchers had proposed as many as 4,000 traits, which were then whittled down to sixteen; but the process of identifying each was unmanageable for psychological practitioners.

The Big Five personality traits are easily remembered in English as the acronym OCEAN: openness, conscientiousness, extraversion, agreeableness, and neuroticism.

Openness is an eagerness to new experiences and ideas. It reflects the state of one's imagination and insight and is often associated with creativity.

Conscientiousness is associated with people who are thoughtful, plan ahead, and exercise good impulse control. They achieve goals through organization and attention to detail.

Extraversion (the opposite of introversion) measures how comfortable one is in social settings or around others. An extravert is fueled by the presence of others.

Agreeableness is manifested through kindness, charitable behavior, and affection. An agreeable person is more willing to help others.

Neuroticism describes one's response to stress and uncertainty. It is expressed in moodiness, sadness, and anxiety.

Each of the Big Five are tracked along a spectrum. One can be more open or more closed, agreeable or disagreeable, neurotic or well-balanced. Combined, they offer a relatively rich measure of the individual.

Now let's contrast the Big Five with how brands appeal to their audience. Most brand communication appeals to triggers along the fight-or-flight/pleasure spectrum. The majority of messages focus on fear/security (the fear of death), the acquisition of material gain, or the attraction of sexual partners. In comparison, this seems rather impoverished and relegated to the most base reptilian stimuli—the id.

One of the great criticisms of social media is how it uses outrage to maintain users' attention. This is an appeal to the reptilian mind, where algorithms filter and provide posts designed to keep the user doom-scrolling for hours.

Perhaps these are vestiges of earlier advertising models of limited channels and mass audiences, when the lowest common denominator was enough for an effective message. But today's environment of algorithmically powered analysis and content generation seems to offer the potential for more-nuanced psychologically complex messages—which are ideal opportunities for brands to contribute to the creation of a richer social environment.

Naomi Osaka is a good example of a marketable athlete, capable of speaking frankly about their struggles, which suggests that people want to hear from people in all their vulnerability and fragility.

Markers like this one for ADP home alarm systems, as seen in the
Ditmas section of Brooklyn, are directed towards feelings of security
and the fear of death.

8 BLACK BOX OR SCIENTIFIC METHOD

Branding is more of an art than a logic-based science.

The amount that a client is willing to pay can be enhanced by maintaining a degree of mystery, presenting oneself as an expert or with a sense of professionalism, or both. Mystery adds intrigue and sexiness. Expertise and professionalism add comfort. It's worth considering because this describes a tension between the role of branding practitioners and client expectations and how that pollutes perceptions of the profession in general.

There was a period of time in the beginning of this century when branding firms described their proprietary processes on their websites. Descriptions were light on details, punctuated by a trademarking symbol, and named so as to fit in with current market lingo, with the goal to place firms on the cutting edge of marketing and design. The only way to learn the process was to hire them.

Over time, as people churned through branding agencies, proprietary processes like journey mapping or positioning frameworks made their way into the general population. Ultimately there was no special process. Just variations on market research, development, and execution, with individualized filters of psychology, data analysis, etc. reflecting the interests or experiences of various players. The names of the steps change but remain basically the same.

More cynical designers at the time saw these brand processes as a way to professionalize the "black box" of design. A black box has a clear input and output, but the internal steps remain opaque. Adding a series of steps, proprietary or not, establishes client expectations and offers benchmarks for accountability and tracking progress.

A clearly defined method also helps clients accept the vagueness of creativity. The early stages of the process are analytical and easily verifiable. But a good portion of the creative stage is unquantifiable and resistant to standardization. One can go through a professional process and still come out with a bad branding system.

Perhaps this is one of the many faults in contemporary branding. A professional practice is designed to create professional results. But effective results don't always present themselves in such an environment. The challenge is to engage all possibilities, regardless of where they came from.

Note:
See 23. Customer Journey, 57. Frameworks.

[1]UNIFY

[2]SIMPLIFY

[3]AMPLIFY

Ken Carbone, Cofounder and Chief Creative Director of the
Carbone Smolan Agency, follows the clearly defined method of
Unify, Simplify, and Amplify.

9 BLURRING

The borders around
and between brands
are porous.

More than any other moment in history, the best description for the spirit of the time is to say that we live in the blur. No other generation is as globally connected; companies continually acquire other companies; and content moves from platform to platform. There is no center. Everything flows. The borders between brands and brand associations are more porous than ever.

All of a sudden, it is not so strange for the Spanish luxury fashion house Balenciaga to collaborate with the American footwear company Crocs. And no one seemed to bat an eye when Louis Vuitton collaborated with Supreme to produce cobranded luggage. These collaborations are meeting points where widely divergent brands coexist equally. And maybe that is where the logic lies. Louis Vuitton could never collaborate equally with Balenciaga. They are too similar, as are its customers. But Crocs could easily collaborate with Supreme because it and its customers share an upstart attitude.

This makes the contemporary brand landscape quite interesting. On one hand, one never knows where the next challenger brand, or brand collaboration, will come from. And, conversely, this blurring opens up territory beyond a brand's basic activity. Where Supreme once seemed to ride the leading edge of the blur—moving beyond skateboards and skater gear into Supreme-branded stepladders and inflatable boats—many other brands have a disregard for the fidelity of what could be considered their foundation.

The combination of a financialized economy and the digital realm has now blurred contours to the point where a transportation company like Uber doesn't own any vehicles. And a hospitality company like Airbnb doesn't own any property. Yet, when we need a ride, we call Uber, and when we need a place to stay, we open the Airbnb app.

This only confirms that brands are nothing more than associations. And just as we can entertain multiple ideas in our mind simultaneously, we can entertain multiple brand associations as well.

Brands are also the symbolic system that binds us together as a society. In effect, we speak through brands. And brands help us speak a complex language in a complex time. When Georgian fashion designer Demna Gvasalia had a runway model wear a DHL T-shirt during a show for his Vetements line, the message had multiple layers. It was a comment on the exclusiveness of high fashion, a critique of consumerism, a joke, and more. Such interplay could happen only once the lines between brands were fully blurred.

A red denim Louis Vuitton/Supreme jacket, designed by Louis Vuitton's menswear artistic director, Kim Jones, with the collaboration blurred seamlessly.

10 BODY AND BRAND

We interact with brands using more than just our eyes and ears.

The focus on a brand's visual and verbal expression most likely persists for two reasons. First, these forms are the easiest qualities to reproduce, easily appearing across the widest range of media. And second, they are representations of the brand, not the brand itself. For the sake of expediency let's call them brand impressions.

A brand experience is something quite different. It is an event that happens in a body, in space, and at a particular time. This means that it occurs in a context that can be adjusted to enhance the experience.

An easy way to approach this opportunity is to think about how things shift. Frank Lloyd Wright planned movement through his buildings so that one would enter a large, open space after going through a tight, compressed passage. This gave a subtle and dramatic release upon entering the room. Similar effects can be triggered by moving from dark to light, from deadened acoustic space into a more acoustically active environment, or simply from carpet onto hardwood floors. These are all be appropriate for a brand aligned with ideas of opportunity, growth, or progress. And if the brand was about safety, relaxation, or focus then the programmed movement would be reversed.

In 2004 Samsung opened a brand showroom at the Time Warner Center in New York City. It was a place where potential customers could try out the products without being pressured to buy anything. The space had a very relaxing atmosphere, literally. The air was charged with negative ions, which may have an activating effect on some physiological systems, stimulate cognitive performance, and reduce symptoms of depression. One felt better immediately upon entering the showroom, which, in turn, helped build a positive brand association in the mind.

Another all-too-common technique is to burn a vanilla-scented candle. Originally deployed in the Morgans Hotel Group properties, founded by Studio 54 owners Steve Rubell and Ian Schrager, it continues to persist. Spaces managed by anyone who might have worked for Morgans or the subsequent Ian Schrager Company will have a slight vanilla scent.

Beyond traditional hospitality techniques, we could take lessons from other disciplines. For example, the American conceptual artist Michael Asher set up focused bursts of air to be felt as someone moved through a gallery space and angled walls and ceilings slightly so as to disorient spatial preconceptions.

Collectively techniques like these can subtly energize a space, which in turn can heighten any associations attributed to the experience and the brand. Instead of passing through yet another overly lit untuned, generic space, the customer is treated to an intentional moment that is more than another "ride" or "attraction." They are offered a fuller sense of presence.

A predominate vanilla scent hung in the air of the now-closed Gramercy Park Hotel's lobby.

11 BRAND ARCHITECTURE

Organizing structure plays an important role in branding.

The general thought behind growth is that it is an overall positive result. A variety of opportunities present themselves, the audience is larger, the brand has a larger presence of mind, and financial returns roll in. But growth also brings complexity. As the number of employees increases, opportunities become more varied, opinions (both internally and externally) diversify, and with all that, the "architecture" of the brand becomes noisier.

This noise is influenced by the initial structure of the brand's origin. For example, Google began as a graduate student research project at Stanford University, which looked to see which webpages were linked to other webpages. Those linkages became the basis for a search algorithm that would then rank based on relevance and behavior.

Because Google's origin was in research and its practical application, employees were encouraged to spend 20 percent of their time actively working on what they thought would benefit the company. As the company grew, the number of daily emails received by one person could be in the hundreds. The need for a searchable, web-based internal email system eventually became Gmail, a now-publicly available service.

Over time, this ethos allowed for a variety of projects ranging from robotics to broadband access to autonomous vehicles to health—each with its own regulatory and economic complexities. While all were logical offshoots from search, it became more of a stretch to group and manage under the name Google. In 2015, the company was reorganized under the name Alphabet, and Google became the internet-based offering of the new entity.

Such a reorganization is known as a brand architecture project. It is intended to give structure and clarity to both internal and external audiences, which in turn can prepare a company for the current (and future) marketplace.

Firms with origins in professional services, like advertising agencies or accounting firms, may find themselves creating new divisions to resolve potential conflicts of interest (serving more than one client within a regulated sector, like banking) or to distinguish specialized offerings, like experiential marketing. In these cases, the multiple redundancies and inefficiencies of separate profit-and-loss lines also call out for a brand architecture process.

This is a situation where the political nature of brand architecture emerges. One of the redundancies in such organizations is the number of stakeholders involved. Each has been rewarded for loyal service and results with a department or division to lead. Each has a clientele and constituency, which needs to be carefully addressed.

In that environment, one quickly realizes that brand architecture is as much social engineering as organizational design. The process of stakeholder interviews serves research, as well as psychological needs. And while there is a need for logic in the final structure, that structure won't operate effectively without the emotional investment of its participants.

FedEx

Express

Home Delivery

Ground

Office

Freight

Trade Networks

FedEx's brand architecture reflects a "branded house" strategy,
where each division logically links to the main company.

BRANDS ARE A TECHNOLOGY

Since Apple is regarded as an exemplary model of an ideal brand, it's easy to think that its technological products define the brand. Actually it's the direct opposite.

Let us begin by thinking about what technology is. Simply put, technology is a means to an end. It is how we effect change on the objects in the world. Therefore, technology is an extension of our bodies. A hammer extends our arm; a telescope extends our vision; and the wheel extends our range.

What technology extends our lived experience? Language.

Language is probably humanity's greatest technology. It allows us to reach beyond our place in space and time, offering a bit of immortality and omnipresence, and it allows us to connect with the interior lives of others. And, since brands are a collection of various languages, both visual and verbal, then branding can be seen as a technology in itself.

The technology of branding is more than an extension of one individual lived experience, but rather it is a proposal—an extension—of a way to live. At its most transactional, that way of life could be as anodyne as a Gatorade way to live. Gatorade, which was scientifically developed in a lab at the University of Florida to quench thirst in sporting events, went from a single recipe to a full range of drinks and chewables targeted for every step of a sporting event. There is a preworkout regime, one during the event, and one for recovery afterward. Given that most Gatorade customers are not high-performance athletes, the storytelling may seem a bit overkill, but it still extends a way of living.

What is remarkable about a brand like Apple is how its products gather together into a coherent point of view. That approach isn't as programmatic as Gatorade but instead makes a claim that digital products should remove speed bumps in the physical world. Beginning with the graphical user interface—followed by the iPod, iTunes, iPhone, app store, Apple Wallet, and Apple ID—Apple's products and services are collectively orchestrated to help the user navigate daily life as easily and fully as possible. The brand is agnostic to each user's individuality but very focused on maintaining a seamless continuity of that personal experience across all products, easily handshaking across every transition.

We know what it is to live "Apple." And we can easily distinguish between living "Apple" and any number of ways of living: living "Android," living "Ikea," or living "Catholic Church." Each way of living has been extended, through the technology of brand, to each of us.

Top: Apple store by the Chicago River in Chicago.
Bottom: Apple store in Liberty Square, Milan.
Two locations separated by an ocean, but united by an
aesthetic point of view.

13 BRANDED UNCONSCIOUS

If we think in images, do we also think in brands?

The introduction of photography set off a chain of events that has profoundly altered the way human beings understand the world both consciously and unconsciously. Photographs decouple image from subject, while paradoxically recording a singular moment. If the image is not retouched or altered, the subject is "real," with the photograph acting as a window into another place and time. We no longer need to see things in person in order to believe.

A series of sequential photographs strung together becomes a motion picture. This allows us to play with time. Film sped up, slowed down, or played backwards opens a whole new degree of understanding. We now have proof whether a running horse continually keeps one hoof on the ground, who crossed a finish line first, or whether a ball was in bounds. Slow motion crashes and falls, depending on the narrative, are either movingly tragic or outrageously comic. Emotions are intensified through this new photographic language or dulled through repetition. And in such a situation, the potential for viewer fatigue requires increasingly heightened visual effects, to the point where the images on screen may need exaggeration in order to feel "real."

This idea of a photographic unconscious was proposed by the German cultural critic Walter Benjamin in the mid-1930s, and, almost a century later, his observations still ring true. And building upon his work, one wonders if there is such a thing as a branded unconscious.

If photographs and moving images are able to convey a sense of events in time, what is it that brands convey? If brands are basically associations held in the mind of the audience, what is the potential nature of that association?

Photographs and moving images allow us to experience distant events or events that happen too slowly or quickly to perceive. In a way, they bring us closer. Closer without the need to travel.

So perhaps brands bring us nearer to an ideal. Nike allows us to feel nearer to athleticism, Disney to magic and happiness, Volvo to safety, and Levi's to our informal selves. Brands allow us to occupy, charge, or approach variations of feelings in a shorthanded way. And much as we speak a language without thinking about every single word, we use the language of brands in a similarly unconscious manner.

But it does serve to remember that while we behave like we control and shape language, it is actually language that controls and shapes us. Brands now control and shape human activity as equally as any other social structure.

This 1878 series of images by English photographer, Eadweard Muybridge, revealed how a galloping horse's hooves did not continually touch the ground; thus expanding our perception of the world. Today brands have a similar revealing effect.

14 CAMPAIGNS

Branding is not advertising.

"Branding" is a relatively vague term. It means different things to different people and, consequently, ends in different results, depending on how the word is defined. And to make things even more cloudy, branding can be done by advertising firms, and advertising can be done by branding firms. There is no border guard between the two camps.

Thus the general public uses "advertising" and "branding" interchangeably.

The difference between advertising and branding is easily described with time. Advertising campaigns are generally tactical, while branding has a wider scope. Advertising works within a more immediate time frame of months, while branding works across years. Advertising is usually done by an agency, while branding is the responsibility of agencies and internal departments together.

A common metaphor used in branding is the clock model. Divide a clock face into three equal sections: 12–4 is prepurchase, 4–8 is purchase, and 8–12 is post-purchase. This is a basic model of the lifespan of customer interaction, often called the "customer journey."

Prepurchase now becomes the main domain of advertising. Actions in this domain are intended to build brand awareness, differentiate from competitors, motivate customer/client action, and make a case for purchase.

Branding, on the other hand, covers all areas of the clock. Prepurchase is product development, production, design, naming, setting up distribution channels, and anything needed to prepare for the ideal transaction. Purchase covers that moment when the product moves from "buy me" to "take me home." This could include ease of selection, speed of delivery, how something is packaged, how it is taken out of the package, putting in the batteries, and turning it on for the first time. And the final area, postpurchase, might cover how a brand offers tech support, resolves returns and exchanges, sells accessories, or connects users to build community.

Advertising is also a quick litmus test of culture. Messaging can be easily tweaked to respond to cultural shifts, while products need longer lead time.

Though it works with a different charter, branding still needs to observe advertising's effects. For example, Colonial American style was trendy in the 1930s, and in that moment, the Early American Old Spice toiletries line was introduced for both women and men. Over the decades, Old Spice maintained their traditional association in both product and advertising, tweaking both product and advertising along the way. But in 2010, advertising agency Wieden + Kennedy developed a wildly successful campaign, which was more sexually humorous than traditionally masculine. The perceptive shift of the brand opened space for line extensions into hair pomades, additional scents, and sport products—and became a lesson in the give-and-take between advertising and branding.

Note:
See 23. Customer Journey.

The clock metaphor of customer interaction. 12–4 is prepurchase,
4–8 is purchase, and 8–12 is postpurchase.

15 CASE STUDIES

Overrelying on the case study model is dangerous.

Because of its widespread usage in business, brand professionals tend to work within the case study model. Developed at the Harvard Business School in the 1920s, the case study model strives to analyze crisis moments in a business history by identifying root causes, actions taken, and ensuing results. The benefits of studying these cases are, in the immediate sense, any insights drawn from group discussion, and, in the indirect sense, the personal connections made through such activities. More than a didactic process, the case study model establishes social connections that establish the student within a larger business tradition, which they then continue. The case study model perpetuates itself.

Studying historical examples may seem like an appropriate approach to business education, but there are inherent flaws. First is the realization that all history is the result of an imposed narrative. Someone had to write that study, and their inherent biases affect how that story was told. The presence of financial data may suggest objectivity, but in reality there is no objectivity. The story is much more nuanced than just the numbers.

And there's more to the situation than the thin sample of an individual case study. Crisis moments are often a cumulative eruption of a series of influences, which requires a rigorous and genealogical (as opposed to historical) investigation. A proper analysis could draw from basically any field, as long as it was appropriate to the topic.

Branding presentations frequently begin with some variation of the case study model: a context is presented, a crisis is identified, a clientele is studied, and an insight is revealed. This becomes the launching point for the agency's proposed plan of action. Speaking the case study language shows that one understands, respects, and is a part of the tradition, which then establishes the context for an appropriate client response.

The case study tradition is a common training ground for presidents, cabinet officials, elected representatives, CEOs—basically, the leaders of the world. And what have they given the world? Climate crisis, fractured politics, and economic inequity are their returns.

So why not move beyond the case study model? Why not open our apertures to take in sociological, anthropological, psychological, philosophical, or other theoretical models? If branding is the realm where audiences interact with products and services, then wouldn't it be equally appropriate for brand professionals to regard them from as many angles as possible?

As life, the world, and culture become more segmented, it seems equally responsible to be open-minded in return. And the case study tradition could stand to be supplemented by any number of disciplines, whether it be sociology, literature, philosophy, or dance. If it can describe a relationship, then it may be applicable in branding.

The Harvard Business School.
Birthplace of the case study model.

Connecting a celebrity with a brand may introduce additional levels of complications.

In a 1958 interview, author Theodore Sturgeon spoke about his revelation after years of defending science fiction against arguments based upon the genre's worst examples. "The Revelation: Ninety percent of everything is crud."

Sturgeon's revelation (also known as Sturgeon's Law) is a good benchmark, one that is especially applicable when looking at advertising. Because 90 percent of advertising is most definitely crud. This includes celebrity advertising, which is both the easiest path to client approval and the laziest form of professional practice.

An example of early celebrity advertising includes a prominent Chesterfield cigarettes series in the 1940s and 1950s featuring actor (and future President of the United States) Ronald Reagan. In this type of advertisement, the celebrity's presence certifies the brand in a nonspecific manner. Frankly, unless the celebrity is an expert in a way that lends deeper credibility, like Tiger Woods for Nike's introduction of golf wear, one celebrity is as good as any other.

There needs to be a logical connection between celebrity and brand. Carlos Santana was a perfect choice to endorse Mesa/Boogie guitar amps. But his line of shoes erodes his brand equity, even if a portion of the proceeds go to charity.

The next level of celebrity endorsement is the brand ambassador. Ideally this is a level where thinking of one immediately evokes the other. Audrey Hepburn's relationship with Hubert de Givenchy is most likely the gold standard of brand ambassadorship. Meeting just before each other became famous, Givenchy dressed Hepburn for 40 years of films and public appearances. Hepburn credited Givenchy's clothes as being "the only ones I feel myself in," and, in return, she gave the brand a sense of easy elegance.

This model, a partnership between friends, has devolved into a ritual where celebrities are robotically asked who they are wearing during red carpet events. The celebrity will gush for a few minutes about how much they love a particular designer, which may be true, but there are probably contractual agreements in place that ensure that they will wear that brand a certain number of times over a set period of time. Obligation over connoisseurship.

Recently a rather curious trend has emerged: the celebrity as brand creative director. One wonders what actual product innovations were introduced during Justin Timberlake's turn as creative director of Bud Light Platinum, or Alicia Keys at BlackBerry, Lady Gaga at Polaroid, or will.i.am at Intel. And believability is stretched when learning that singer Selena Gomez has a line of handbags for Coach and a line of cookware for Our Place. Unless it's rapper and cannabis expert Snoop Dogg unveiling a new line of products in Leafs By Snoop, relinquishing product development to a celebrity is rarely a good strategy.

Rapper and cannabis expert, Snoop Dogg, is the owner of the Leafs By Snoop line of medical and recreational marijuana-related products.

CHARACTER

A common trope in branding and design is to describe the practice as a version of storytelling. This most likely is a confluence of thinking about the customer journey—a kind of narrative in itself—and the way in which lessons are often conveyed. The problem with such thinking is that it reduces things to a procedural level. The audience is taken through a logical process that ends in some sort of engagement.

But logic is rarely the driving force behind human decision making. It takes too long to compile facts, make a rational analysis, and decide upon an action—especially when considering all the decisions made throughout a typical day. Emotions act as a decision-making detour. And emotions are usually the way in which the impasses of logical arguments are overcome.

One of the great tensions in the process of film screenwriting lies between character and narrative. It is considered better to write a plot where a character struggles with conflict or goes through a transformative process. The audience becomes more engaged if it can identify with the people portrayed on screen. And the more engaging a character is, the more it becomes a cultural benchmark. Many of us know a Ferris Bueller type, have worked for a Miranda Priestly, or have stumbled into a situation like a Forrest Gump.

Human beings are hard-wired for character. We easily see faces or patterns in ambiguous fields, whether they be visual or behavioral, in a phenomena known as "parcidolia." And those patterns are the building blocks of character.

Character helps us navigate personal relationships. We understand the people in our lives through their personalities, and then use those personalities to regulate our interactions. Personal narratives most definitely have an effect on character development, but our connections are built from the mental associations of an individual's makeup.

So perhaps it is best to think of brands as character driven. Allowing a brand to develop a distinctive character allows for flexibility as markets and audiences change—while maintaining a sense of continuity. The essence of a character, and the expectations of that character, can remain stable as the world around it changes.

For example, the early version of the British Broadcasting Corporation (BBC) had a monolithic upscale tone, a way of speaking, and a specific kind of programming. But decades of reorganization and expanding, plus competition from independents like ITV and pirate radio, are now reflected in a multifaceted, multiregional array of programming that continues to adhere to a particular set of standards. In other words, the world has changed, but the BBC character remains.

Pareidolia is the phenomenon where human beings see faces or patterns in ambiguous fields.

COMFORT AND DISRUPTION

Out of all the modalities of branding, the one receiving much recent attention is disruption. This conforms with the general consensus that, in order to be noticed, a brand needs to stand out dramatically from the competition. And that is done by either opening up a new market or finding a way to exploit profit/margin differences.

Yes, disruption is the goal when developing and introducing a brand. Some sort of "unique selling proposition" is a basic marketing requirement. But this overlooks how our relationships with brands are built upon comfort.

If brands are more psychological connections than anything else, then they need to somehow conform to the customer's life. This could be done by removing barriers in the customer's day-to-day experience, adding efficiencies, or adjusting economies—basically making people feel comfortable.

There is an argument for a deeper appreciation of comfort. It is the background against which innovation appears, and it is the context from which meaning is created.

Disruption is a phenomenon that plays at the edges. We receive sensations outside-in: through our eyes, ears, skin, nose, and mouth. And comfort is basically the expectation of sensory continuity, where we can expect things in the next short period of time to be generally the same as they were in the previous. But if we experience a different sensation, one counter to expectations, then that is the transition from comfort to disruption.

We perceive disruption from the inside-out because consciousness is a mental activity directed toward something. When a brand is "disruptive," we have perceived it and determined it to be different from the usual sensory input. And that sense of difference is measured against previous experiences, ones seen as comfortable.

It would be a nightmare to always exist in a state of constant stimulation. The mental activity would be exhausting. A continual modulation between comfort and disruption allows the shock of the new to be assimilated into the everyday.

We constantly measure social belonging on the spectrum from comfort to disruption. We speak the language of others, not one of our own unique and disruptive invention. And that connection gives us comfort. We feel anxiety in situations where we don't speak the language—ones where we don't belong.

Trusted brands relieve anxiety by adopting a common language—aesthetics, usage, behavior, etc.—and fitting comfortably into the customer's life. Their introduction may have been a shock, but their longevity derives from comfort.

The tension between comfort and disruption is constantly changing. All design may look the same for the time being, but eventually as the innovative becomes the norm, and with historical distance, we are able to register the migration of design, of brands, and of ways of living.

Top: Door knobs were standard hardware in the United States for a century.
Bottom: After the Americans with Disabilities Act of 1990, the door lever displaced the door knob and has become the preferred choice.

One should explore all proposed directions and their complete outcomes.

Working in branding requires more than learning how to design a visual identity system, name a product, or devise a strategic platform. These are ideas. And anyone can have an idea. The real challenge is in getting someone else, whether client or audience, to accept that idea and then act upon it.

Besides real-life experience in building and presenting multiple brands, there are other venues where one can build the skill of "selling" a brand. One of the most effective skills is acting—improvisational acting, to be specific. "Improv," as it's known, has no prewritten script; instead, improv builds upon a collective agreement to accept each other's proposals, to listen closely to others, and to be present in the moment. In other words, anyone performing in improv has to commit to the bit.

Committing to the bit means to fully immerse oneself in the development of whatever is being created to follow through all the ramifications of any proposition, and to imagine oneself as an authentic inhabitant within that structure. The results may be ridiculously funny, profoundly touching, or anything in between. But because they come from an individual's unique presence, and not a preplanned script, they are often wildly creative.

Committing to the bit also means engaging without hesitation. Presenting an idea halfway allows doubt and fear to grow in the minds of all involved. Doubt and fear are omnipresent. There is no need to allow them any more mental space.

Like learning the guitar, riding a bike, and (obviously) branding, the act of *doing* helps one learn improv. And one gets better by doing it often. The only way to prepare beforehand is to read, listen, and see as much as possible in as many different subjects as possible: history, economics, politics, culture, language, art, etc. Improv—and (obviously) branding—is not about one thing; it is about everything. The more references one can draw from, the richer the palette, the better the outcome.

While helpful in selling, committing to the bit is also helpful when developing a brand. Software development has a term, "dogfooding," to describe the use of a product that one is building. One "eats their own dogfood." While this is good general practice for anyone creating a product, it is not fully throwing oneself into the experience of what it is to be the user. To do that, one needs to fully commit to the bit, and walk, talk, think, eat, and live like the user. Inhabiting this role, without hesitation, builds understanding and empathy of the user or audience. And ideally, this sense of understanding and empathy will continue throughout all aspects of the brand.

Notes:
See 69. Professionalism Second.
Dr. Tom Guarriello frequently counsels students in the School of Visual Arts Masters in Branding program to "commit to the bit."

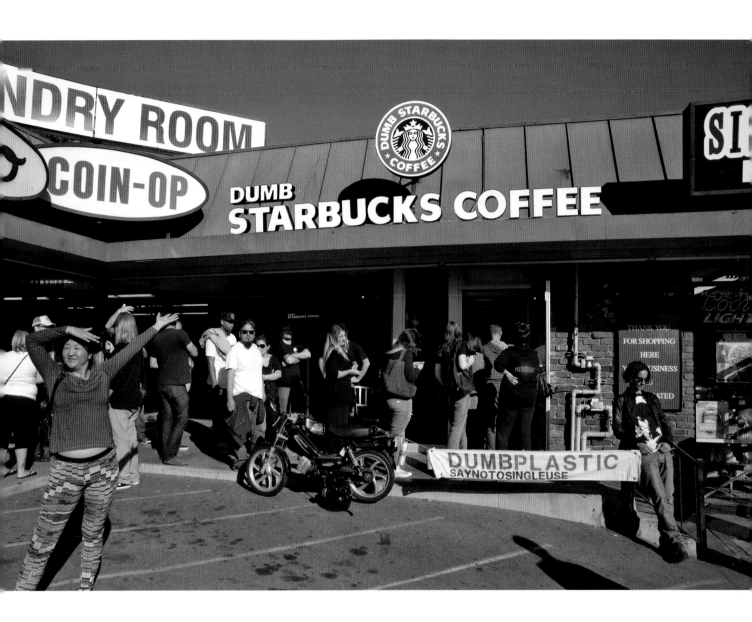

Dumb Starbucks in Los Angeles, California, was a 2014 project by comedian Nathan Fielder, which explored the fair use of copyrighted material as parody.

All the best things come from some degree of conflict.

Conflict seems to be the very nature of the universe; even down to the atomic level. In his *On the Nature of Things*, Roman philosopher-poet Lucretius, the first Roman to write about atoms, saw this metaphor in the action of dust motes in sunlight:

> *"For atoms, since they wander the void, must all*
> *be driven along either by their own weight*
> *or perhaps by striking another. They often meet,*
> *colliding at high speed and then at once*
> *spring wide apart…*
> *All atoms of matter are constantly in motion…"*

There is a conceptual connection between thinking and conflict. Keeping with Latin origins, the roots of the words "cogitate" (to think deeply) and "conflict" have similar origins. Cogitate from co- (together) and "agitare" (to shake); and conflict from "co"- and "fligere" (to strike).

It is in meeting, clashing, and disagreeing that the best ideas are revealed. But this isn't to say that all such interactions need to be acrimonious. Conflict can be constructive, but only when participants are honest, receptive to criticism, and able to see criticism as a gift.

Contemporary culture is rife with the creeping passivity of unexamined open-mindedness. In this case, all paths are equal, all points of view are valid, and we "agree to disagree." Being open-minded and inclusive is good but only if we acknowledge and are transparent about individual differences, limitations, and motivations. This comes from the ability to articulate one's values, something crucial to individuals and brands.

Human resources departments prefer to file conflict under "avoid under all circumstances," when instead it may come from the passion of a talented team member—who might be better supported than written up. And conflict stemming from dissatisfied customers may be the result of a faulty design or standard. In both cases, using brand or company values as a dispassionate lens—regardless of how inconvenient it may be—may turn conflict into a stimulus for growth.

This way, conflict—one of the most basic of human experiences—becomes an important ingredient in the articulation, development, and delivery of a brand. Embraced as a resource, conflict leads to solutions and eventually reveals the nature of anything from the audience's desire, the state of the market, the competitive set, and even the brand itself.

Note:
Lucretius. *On the Nature of Things*. Translated by Frank O. Copley. 1977.
W. W. Norton & Company, Inc., New York, New York. London.

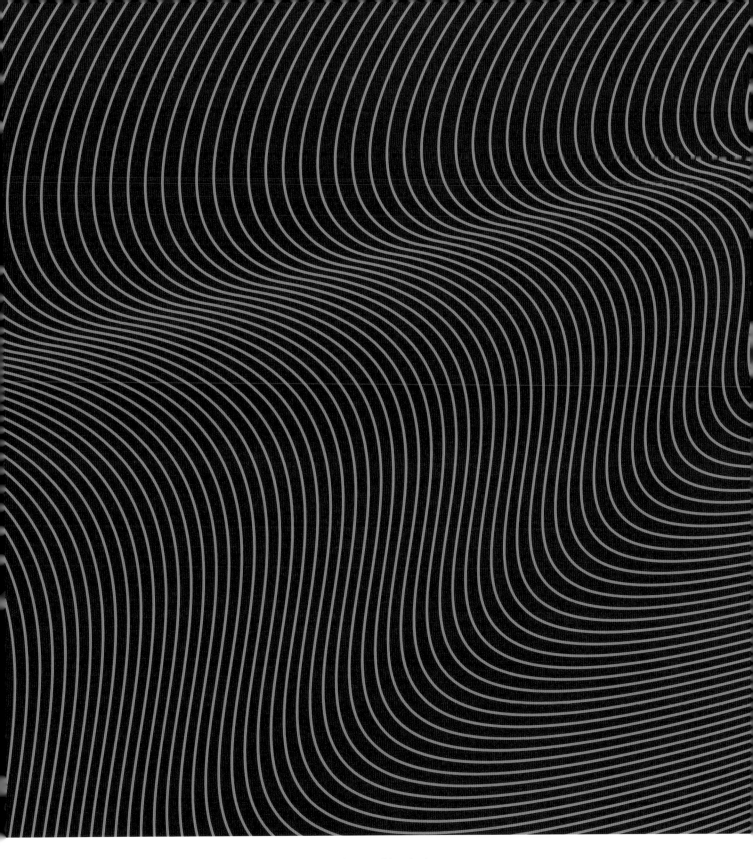

Complementary colors appear on opposite sides of the traditional color wheel. When mixed, they cancel each other out and produce gray. When placed next to each other, they can create vibrant visual effects.

Meaning isn't meaning without context.

Like many revered disciplines, branding can be defined by its vagueness.

Medicine, by its interdisciplinary nature, is vague. There are no sharp boundaries around the diagnosis of disease. How much are the psychological, familial, or regional histories to be taken into consideration? What is the role of mindset in patient recovery, and how can it be measured?

In that light, one begins to understand branding as another discipline born from, and operating out of, vagueness. There seem to be no limits to its territory. The early perception of branding as a combination of strategic positioning, visual identity, packaging, and tone of voice have now grown to entail search engine optimization (SEO) and algorithmic approaches, the role of corporate social responsibility, employee onboarding, and conflict resolution. All human, and at times nonhuman, behavior sits within the purview of branding.

But this begins to sound almost messianic, if not sloppy. Designer Massimo Vignelli was fond of saying, "Design is one." This might be a comforting bromide for designers working in a world ruled by the bottom line, but it doesn't help non-practitioners understand the benefits of an attentive approach to design.

The general view of branding speaks about attracting and maintaining customers while maintaining a unique identity. While correct, it overly focuses on results and returns on investment. No wonder mentions of branding are frequently met with deep cynicism. We are more than just shoppers.

The task, then, is to quickly describe the process of branding, in an open manner, without dropping to the bottom line of customer retention and increased profits.

This is a world of branded objects. We speak in brands, surround ourselves with brands, decide through brands, and set life goals aided by brands. Our context is brands. So perhaps that becomes a way to define the branding profession and its activities. If medicine is concerned with health, then branding is concerned with context.

Branding has both analytical and generative aspects. Simply put: branding is a discipline where practitioners analyze existing contexts then develop new contexts that their clients may authentically and distinctively inhabit.

The word "context" is used vaguely here on purpose. Because branding's territory is constantly expanding, the number of contexts does as well. Beyond the marketplace, there are linguistic, political, technological, sociological, and aesthetic ramifications to the presence of brands in contemporary culture.

The benefit of such an approach, besides underscoring the market value of a brand, is to give, for lack of a better word, an inevitability that is less about the creator's ego and more about an effort to connect with other people. The brand simply fits its context.

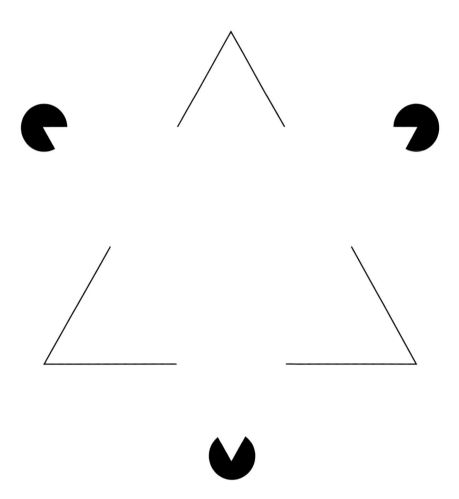

The Kanizsa triangle, named after the Italian psychologist and artist
Gaetano Kanizsa, evokes a white shape in a vague context.

Everyone who works in branding has a craft.

If brands are the expression of interdisciplinary activity then the people who develop, build, distribute, and maintain those brands need to be as unsiloed as possible. In every studio, agency, and factory one finds a variety of personalities all working towards a common goal. And within each of those situations, power dynamics usually contribute to a situation where one member of the group feels alienated or unappreciated at one time or another. While regrettable, it is natural human behavior, one often driven by unexamined assumptions.

There are inherent associations and expectations ascribed to various job titles and functions. To a certain extent, these assumptions create efficiencies. If one is on the financial side, they are expected to have particular analytical and logical abilities, which are different from the analytical logic associated with a strategist.

Definitions also give people excuses to not participate in the brand's full development. While there is no rule preventing someone on the factory floor from proposing a new product, it's easier to just let the product development team fill that need.

The problem here is that people are siloed according to their tasks. If you are a designer, then design is your task. If you are a manager, then your task is management. You are limited to your duty.

But what if we saw people by how they experience and interpret the world? In this case everyone's "craft" becomes the filter through which they contemplate things. Craft ceases to be a precious possession to be protected at all costs. It ceases to be a differentiator between "us" and "them" and ultimately becomes the bridge across which one can connect with the larger world.

The letterpress printer Amos Kennedy Jr. once said, "I do not believe that I am mastering the craft so much as I am allowing the craft to explain the workings of the universe—the workings of the universe and the connections that make the universe flow."

We need to redefine what it means to have a craft and then begin seeing teammates as equally skilled within their own craft tradition, one that expands how the collective team explains "the working of the universe" to each other and to its audience.

This approach has the potential to open new avenues of creativity, carve out new territories, and identify new audiences, both for the brand and the cultural landscape in which it sits. And perhaps reconfirming why we do what we do—reminding us that the product of our work is the material that mediates human relationships.

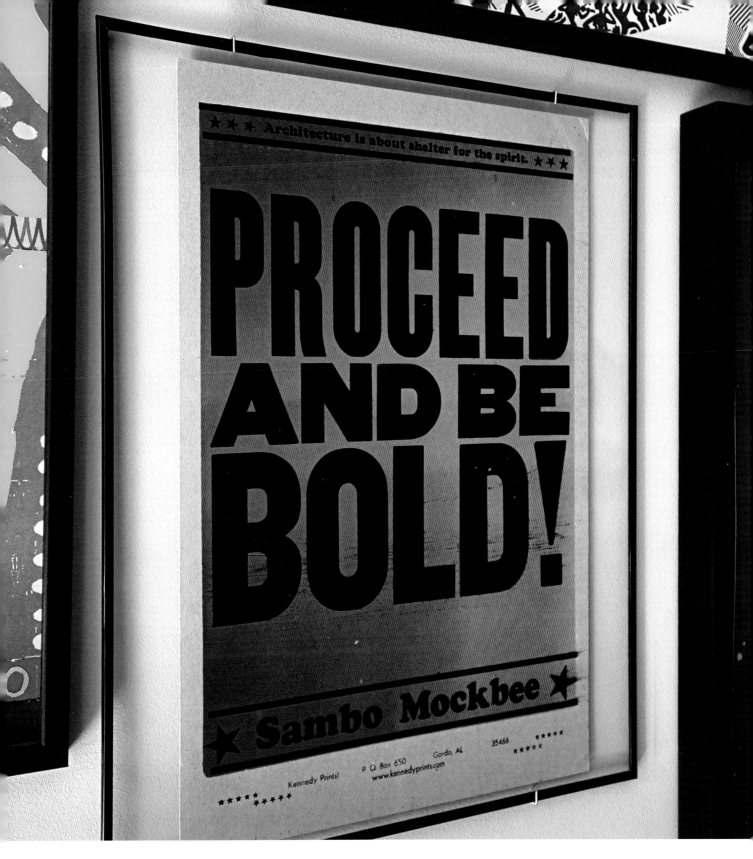

Amos Kennedy Jr.'s "Proceed and Be Bold!" poster; as seen in the author's collection.

The customer journey is a useful tool in branding.

One of the most fundamental framing tools used in branding is the customer journey. It helps describe the transformation of a person from potential customer into a purchaser, then a user, and then ideally an advocate. Measuring these steps against the brand's offerings allows for the development of touchpoints to guide people through and enhance this process. The tool also shifts focus toward the customer's experience and defines goals for each interaction.

Oxford Corporate Consultants (now OxfordSM) is credited with developing the customer journey framework during a 1998 engagement with Eurostar, operators of the London-to-Paris rail service running under the English Channel. At the time, Eurostar had been in business for about five years and was expanding their website ticketing and customer offerings. And with such a complex variety of governments, cultural contexts, freight, and leisure customers, plus contracts across different legal systems, a tool like the customer journey was probably a welcome framing device.

There may be variations in the number of steps, or their names, but the customer journey follows a standard pattern. First is an awareness of the brand, whether by word of mouth, advertising, or seeing someone with the product or brand. This sparks a curiosity about the item/brand.

Once a person is aware of the brand, they need to learn more about it, perhaps through advertising or web searches, reading reviews, or trying out the product (either in store or for a trial period). Then the next step of the journey is the transaction: a purchase, signing up, or becoming a member.

Depending on the product or service, engaging with or using the brand is sometimes tied to conflict resolution or customer service. In any case, this is the longest duration of time to establish the brand's reputation. From there, the journey could transition into advocacy or circle back into another transaction.

While a powerful framework, one should take care not to see the customer journey as a transactional and cumulative progression. At every stage, external forces (cultural, reputational, etc.) can divert away from ideal outcomes. In every case, the customer journey is more of a checklist, or rough guide, than a perfect recipe.

Note:
See 66. Permission.

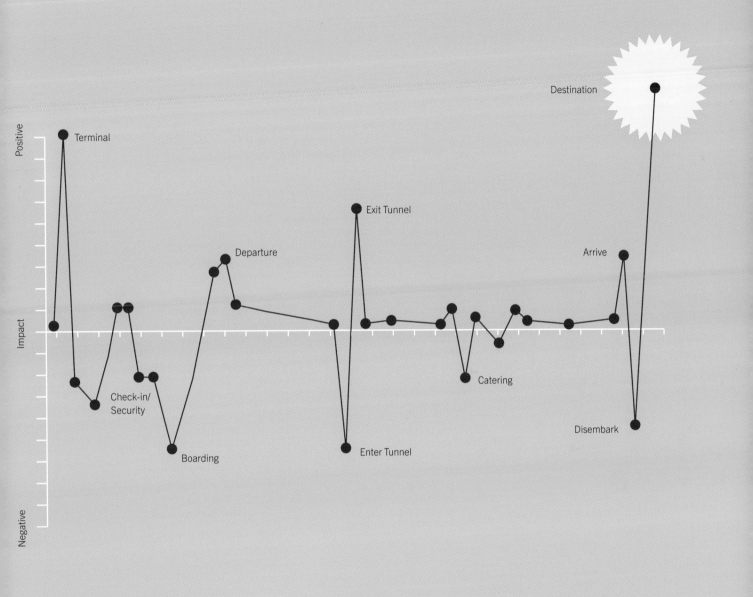

Positive

Impact

Negative

Terminal

Check-in/
Security

Boarding

Departure

Enter Tunnel

Exit Tunnel

Catering

Arrive

Disembark

Destination

A version of Oxford Corporate Consultants' 1998 customer journey
map for Eurostar.

Don't overlook how your
brand is delivered.

Our material culture is under continual erosion by the digital realm. Physical objects that were once common—maps, video cameras, paper tickets—are giving way to digital counterparts. As this process continues, and as companies increasingly disentangle the building blocks of their products across a wider variety of licensed services and servers, the manner in which a brand is delivered has never been more important. Additionally the rise of digital markets (Amazon, for example) and direct-to-consumer brands now adds the potential for another brand touchpoint.

In the digital realm, brands need to consider load time. Fast networks create expectations that something will appear on screen almost instantaneously. And the thirty seconds that people used to allow for buffering and loading has diminished to a mere fraction of that time. This has an effect on design. Typefaces may be selected according to how the target audience aligns with webtype servers. Moving image files may be hosted on third-party platforms, and material may be formatted for optimum results when shared in social media.

Brands also need to balance the constantly changing formats of new devices. Smartphones created a mobile-first approach to webpage design, and one can be confident that the next widely adapted delivery system will have the same effect. Cumulatively, we have an environment where a responsive webpage allows for typefaces that aren't supported on a particular device to be substituted or altered in system settings to accommodate an individual's visual acuity and reflects a brand's behavioral and verbal character more consistently than its visual identity system.

In the material world, the death of traditional retail means more packages arriving on consumer doorsteps. To make them less appealing to potential thieves, some companies print their graphics on the inside of the box. When done well—quality printing on good cardboard stock—the effect can be elevating, like discovering some treasure. This works quite well for a wine or luxury clothing brand but might be overkill for an Amazon toilet paper subscription. The goal is to enhance the brand without seeming like an ordinary marketing exercise, like including a cheap gift-with-purchase or coupon for future purchases.

Comparing digital or physical means of delivery reveals a tension across the two. Digital delivery concerns itself with speed and efficiency where physical delivery inherently has a wider possibility for surprise and delight through materiality, shifts in texture, or smell. The challenge is channeling, and narrowing, the open potential of physical delivery—fully, sensorially, experiencing the moment—in a digital environment.

Who Gives a Crap packages their bamboo-based toilet paper in decorative wrapping and puns. The only plastic used is the tape that seals the shipping box.

Sometimes a brand's meaning is immediate. Sometimes it takes a while.

We live in a chaotic universe. There is no meaning to anything other than the one we attribute. So why do we collectively live in a world where we pretend that brands, logos—even materials, shapes, and colors—all have inherent meaning to them? Gold does not mean "rich" or "luxury;" it just is gold. Black does not mean "alternative" or "witch;" it is just black. And if one lines up samples of gold or black, one can see that there are yellow golds and blue golds and warm blacks and cool blacks. There are no absolutes to these phenomena, just like there are no absolutes to what they mean. Gold is a range, black is a range, luxury is a range, and alternative is a range.

So then, what do brands mean? Basically, nothing. They mean nothing in and of themselves because they are given meaning through their use and the associations we ascribe to them. One that differs from person to person and migrates over time and contexts.

Meaning is a product of our anthropomorphic projection upon a chaotic universe. Our consciousness, and ultimately our language, was probably built off of binary differences like present/absent, near/far, bigger/smaller, dark/light, hot/cold, etc. And since what is bigger than me may be smaller than you, or what is chilly to me may be too warm for you, we quickly understand the relativity and slipperiness of those binary differences.

Yet meaning comes from difference. And since difference is contextual, the idea of truth itself is also relative. There is no one truth but a momentary truth revealed in a particular moment—like coming upon a clearing in a dark forest and then coming upon another clearing and then another. All true moments. All different.

Within the consideration of branding, this becomes another appreciation in how audiences are really the ones who manifest a brand. And that brand meaning isn't fixed. One's perception can shift over time. Change in a brand's behavior, the cultural climate in which it sits, or even the actions of an employee all can shift a brand's meaning.

This is something that the French philosopher Jacques Derrida called "différance"—a play on the similarities of the French words for "differ" and "defer." For him, deferred meaning described the ongoing play of signifieds and signifiers. An active field that requires the branding practitioner to listen differently—beyond the transactional—and to see their work as a dialogue.

Strategy is often defined as deliberate differentiation. But in our chaotic universe model, difference becomes, in a sense, a handle that our consciousness can grasp. An assist rather than an insist.

The philosopher, Gilles Deleuze, offers an interesting way of thinking about brands. "Instead of something distinguished from something else, imagine something which distinguishes itself."

Cultural strategy is more important than digital strategy.

There is a general tendency in creative agencies to view innovations in the digital realm as mystical and magical. Our attraction to the new can be seen across design and marketing history—from optical innovations in photography to digital typesetting, Photoshop, spinning Flash logos, bootstrapped web pages, and machine learning. But the work still begins with the idea.

With society's entrance into the internet age, the role of strategist began to be split between the Harvard Business School case study model and the new, exotic digital strategist—both having responsibilities that continue to be difficult to define and specific to the company. Originally no more than "having something to do with wireframes or something," digital strategy now concerns itself with algorithmic approaches to user experience and data.

This mirrors what happened in the creative department. An art director was once the person with a network of photographers, illustrators, and other resources. They contacted the person they felt was best for a project and arranged the engagement. Today that position has been disambiguated into an art director who determines what things will look like, an art buyer who maintains the contact list of approved vendors, and a resource person who negotiates contracts and payment.

The fallout of that separation was that art directors no longer have the kind of visual literacy that naturally came from having to know a full range of visual colleagues. Their knowledge now tends to be influenced through social media feeds, industry press, and consumer media.

There might be a lesson to be learned here and an opportunity to redefine strategy roles. The division between a "traditional strategist" and digital strategist is false. Both analyze situations and propose responses, so it's all strategy.

But if one were to create a subspecialty that plays a strategic role, perhaps there's room for a social strategist. It wouldn't be a trend forecaster but rather more like a human seismograph tracking the increasing frequency of vibe shifts reverberating through society.

There is a tendency to use anthropological and sociological observation to track consumption. But that feels somehow limited. The social strategist would frame their observations through psychological, philosophical, and sociological models in an attempt to track mindsets as they develop. The people who do similar work today are cultural critics and public intellectuals like Malcolm Gladwell or Douglas Rushkoff.

A good critic places phenomena in culture, which seems to align nicely with branding. The Canadian anthropologist Grant McCracken proposed in 2009 that agencies have a Chief Culture Officer position (looking externally), which differs from any internal Company Culture Office (i.e., human resources). Given the speed with which culture now moves, this seems even more relevant today.

A sampling of critics and intellectuals whose work traces the reverberations of society.
Top row, left to right: Malcolm Gladwell, Li Edelkoort, Walter Benjamin
Bottom row, left to right: Slavoj Žižek, Susan Sontag, Douglas Rushkoff

DISAGGREGATED DATA

One of the analytical tools of the COVID pandemic was the generation and usage of rich data. The speed of how the virus spread across the world—compounded by political inconsistency, the ease of travel, and varying degrees of access to vaccines and therapies—created a high degree of uncertainty and flux. And, generally, many public health protocols were based on aggregated data like the percentage of intensive care units available, infection rates, and overall amount of the population who had been tested.

Aggregated data produces an easy-to-understand number when setting public policy, but pandemics affect different subpopulations differently. And aggregated data doesn't always offer nuance, which could best direct a targeted, preventative response. That required disaggregated data, gathered at the individual level, and filtered so as to accurately represent populations by neighborhood, frequency of public transportation usage, income/education level, disability, ethnic origin, etc. Armed with that information, health officials could get a grasp on the complex variations within different socio-economic groups, and then measure effectiveness for each approach, whether it be testing, vaccination, or masking.

For decades, the largest branding and advertising agency holding companies have maintained divisions engaged in a version of research based on disaggregated data. Their international footprint allows them to track populations in each country, over time, and measure their impressions of market sectors ranging from services to products to organizations. From there, insights can see how, for example, small families with white collar parents making US$150,000 or more have thought about a specific bank for the past decade. Those feelings can comprise a range of impressions from trustworthiness to aggressiveness to sexiness. Each insights group has its own individualized group of factors, and they can track shifts across a range of demographic populations.

As algorithms and machine learning continue to evolve the richness of disaggregated data, brands have access to more detailed information about the results from, and needs of, certain groups within their audience. This allows for more effective or responsive offers, which improves efficiencies and delivery time.

While both forms of data are essential to understanding how a brand sits and performs within a market context, disaggregated data is useful when diagnosing deeper issues such as disparate adaptation rates across populations or decline in brand loyalty. But regardless of how it's composed, all data needs to be interpreted with sensitivity. This is the difference between observation and insight.

Aggregated data does not fully reveal the focused details of relations
or context.

Brands and branding are more than a way to make money.

Any tool, whether it is an instrument or a method, is inherently neutral. It has no ambition, is indifferent to its application, and maintains no ethical stand. It just is ready at hand, waiting to be used.

A visit to Google's Ngram Viewer shows that the phrases "product branding" and "branding" both have a noticeable uptick in the 1940s and then show explosive growth in usage beginning in the late 1980s. Since that time the art, craft, and science of branding has matured and become more effective. Every step of the customer journey is now parsed and closely inspected; consumer data is sifted through all variations of criteria; and strategists explore a burgeoning feed of case studies for insights and inspiration. The amount of material on branding grows exponentially.

Specific branding techniques—disaggregated data, for example—can either be used to better understand consumer needs or be used to specifically target advertising. The former can promote human existence; the latter can potentially destroy the fabric of civil society.

Branding, the profession and everything it serves, can exist only if there is an audience. So common sense suggests that everyone working in branding should direct their efforts towards the continued presence of that audience. All actions reverberate into the future, often with unintended consequences, and that moment of engagement is one brief moment in a series of events impacting the larger world.

The semiotician and human/computer interaction expert Dr. Mihai Nadin frequently states that the intentions of the programmer come through in the program. This notion, not restricted to computer science, applies to any programmatic endeavor: politics, education, jazz festivals, and, of course, branding.

If one could zoom out for an overview of branding presentations around the world, one would be struck by their positive outlook. No sane person wants to approve a project that will destroy their future endeavors, so everything is dressed in breathless optimism. But, regrettably, that optimism may be too narrowly focused on short-term advantages at the expense of lingering effects.

A good place to start is to redefine the rationale for most brand development, which is profit. An account of profits at a moment of time is capital while a flow of transactions through a period of time is income. The word "economy" describes a social domain that manages the production and use of scarce resources. What would happen if we expanded that definition beyond financial profit and considered how branding could address multiple flows of ecological, social, and health transactions? Expanding the branding domain beyond a traditional customer journey, which pivots around the transaction, could have a market-expanding effect.

Note:
See 27. Disaggregated Data, 23. Customer Journey.

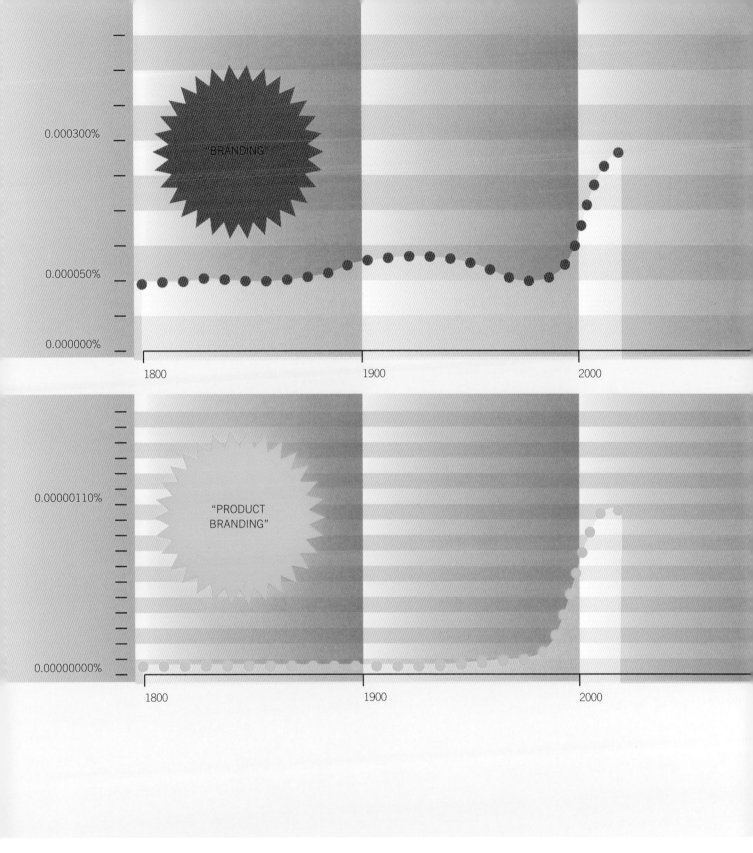

Results from Google's Ngram Viewer for the phrases "branding"
(top) and "product branding" (bottom).

Brand audits are
crucial.

The presence of experts in our physical lives—dentists, doctors, nurses—offers the kind of input that is built from a wider experience than just us alone. This outsider perspective is advantaged in that it allows for a greater objectivity in its evaluation. In a sense, the expert acts as a dispassionate referee.

The word "audit" carries negative connotations due to its use in accounting and taxes. To be audited by a government official or oversight party is to be subject to an opinion that may have difficult financial ramifications. Financial audits, like cavities in teeth, can be uncomfortable to resolve. But an audit is a powerful tool in the development and management of a brand. And as a brand grows into new markets and expanded offerings, audits become more of a necessary step.

Engagements with a new brand agency typically begin with some sort of brand audit, whether requested by the client or done as due diligence. All available materials and interactions, known as touchpoints, are gathered and evaluated against the brand's stated values and standards. Additionally a competitive audit can evaluate a brand against others in the marketplace in order to identify best practices.

Once a brand grows to a point where there are too many touchpoints for an easy evaluation—growth across regions, languages, and demographics—regular brand audits become a management necessity. This can range from determining whether the correct colors are used in all situations or various behaviors properly express brand values to possible legal ramifications of architectural installations. But this has to be balanced with regional specifics. Banks in Japan present gifts to customers who open new or additional accounts while banks in the United States no longer feel compelled to. Stores in Moscow are allowed to have broken steps at the front door because they were built before local liability laws, and to repair them would expose that step to the updated requirements. In that specific location, a broken step may not necessarily be seen as a detriment to the brand experience. In this case, an arrangement needs to be made between the needs and expectations of specific audiences and the needs and expectations of the brand.

Multiregional or global brand audits can be part of a company-wide unification effort. They can fuel internal marketing awards, be used for employee and partner education, and build connections between offices. The ideal result of a well-executed audit is a coherent brand that feels appropriate for its local audience. And probably the best example of variety within coherence is Sesame Street programming. Characters are different across markets, but the basic lessons of human dignity remain the same.

Top: The characters Bert and Ernie on the original American television show *Sesame Street*
Bottom: The character Baaji on *SimSim Humara*, the Pakistani version of *Sesame Street*.

There is more to brands
than their visual identity.

Let's consider man-made systems. Electrical systems power human life and activity. Transportation systems enable economic and social interaction. Water and sewage systems are crucial to the health of people living in proximity to each other.

While systems might initially appear neutral, their existence allows for potential applications beyond the original intent. Electrical systems were needed for the development of computer technology and changed how we entertain ourselves. Transportation systems allowed for recreational travel and the idea of driving for pleasure. And water/sewage systems changed land use patterns, which, in turn, had a profound effect on the environment.

So man-made systems also reframe how we see the world.

In the mid-twentieth century, graphic design systems were the building blocks for what became known as corporate identity. One started with a logo, then selected a typeface and a color palette, arranged them in a consistent manner, and then applied that look and feel to stationery, business cards, the sides of trucks, signage, and so on. The design system helped identify an organization, while the organization's goods, services, and behaviors contributed to how the general public felt about it.

But the development of information technology changed how we view design. Audiences are familiar with a wide variety of images and other visual elements. Digital media introduced motion, time, and sound. And businesses began to see design as a tactic within a cohesive brand system.

Corporate identity designers were then required to move beyond the creation of a perfect artifact, like the perfect logo or the perfect package, into the creation of an ecosystem (physical, digital, perceptual, and emotional) intended to "hang together" so that the audience can develop the sort of mental response we now call a "brand."

And since a brand is the association held in a person's mind, this means that there is now an expanded opportunity for expression. The expression of a personality, a character, or a point of view helps this ecosystem hang together as a coherent brand. Feelings, in all their ambiguity, are as important to a brand as a good logo, if not more so.

Current brand practice aspires to use brand values (conveyed through character, personality, etc.) as a way to differentiate. And these elements traditionally come from the strategy side. But the reality is that creative exploration also plays a vital role in the development of a brand personality.

In order to become more effective in today's world, anyone working in branding needs to be comfortable in this hybrid and ambiguous space. They need to look beyond their expertise to see how their work "feels" in a larger social context, as well as develop an ability to connect to the general public through these feelings.

Two divergent brand ecosystems in 2018 that feel different from each other.
Top: The original pride flag, seen in Berlin at the 40th Christopher Street Day.
Bottom: Masked Kashmiri protesters with the flag of the Islamic State (ISIS).

Brands need to equally address their external and internal audiences.

While the conversation about brands tends to focus on the audience, employee engagement—aligning employees to a brand's values and personality—is also a crucial factor. It ensures consistency across all customer interactions, reinforces brand associations, and may help build efficiencies.

And it can also be the connective glue that holds a brand together, especially a brand with a wide range of products.

The traditional approach to employee engagement is to define the brand's values—sometimes called the brand pillars. These are usually written and agreed upon by committee, with every word vetted against its strategic purpose. Each decision made by, and for, the company is then measured against those values.

Sometimes brand values are distilled into a purpose statement. A notable example would be Nike's purpose of "breaking barriers." Clothing and footwear is conceived and designed so customers can transcend their current physical state into a healthier, more athletic existence. And one would hope that the same purpose would apply to how products are packaged and delivered: with clearly designed, easy-to-read labeling and easy-to-open packaging.

How would "breaking barriers" apply to the hiring process or when an employee leaves the company? Perhaps the human resources department would endeavor to create an application process that initially obscured names, neighborhoods, ages, or other specific details, which could fuel biases. Perhaps the company could aid those leaving the company in finding new positions or training.

In everyday operation, "breaking barriers" could focus interactions between employees and customers or vendors. The goal with a customer would not center on the transaction but rather to help them reach a higher level of activity. And "breaking barriers" with a vendor could be collaborating to help them to act with greater efficiency or profit. Annual employee reviews, when measured against "breaking barriers" could be richer than just tracking sales or efficiency.

It quickly becomes clear how employee engagement is extremely important to the brand's health, an aspect that is worth continual and nonrepetitive reinforcement. Unfortunately it is an expensive step frequently streamlined into a one- or two-day "onboarding."

Employee engagement is a continual process of cultural reinforcement. The goal is to have employees "be" the brand without having to "think" the brand first. To have customers feel like they're dealing with a reliable human being who is part of a coherent group, instead of a robot reciting a script.

Actively aligning all levels of employees to a brand's values and personality ensures consistency across customer interactions, reinforces brand associations, and may help build efficiencies.

The tetrad is a useful analytical tool.

In 1964 when the Canadian philosopher and media theorist Marshall McLuhan wrote that "the medium is the message," it was in the context of describing the perceptive changes that follow the introduction of new media or technologies. To McLuhan, the message (or character) of something like television was its societal effect—how it reconfigured human behavior and expectations across business, culture, politics, and beyond. Conversely television's content was easily grasped and relatively inconsequential to how we understand the world, regardless of whether it came in the form of Saturday morning cartoons or political debates.

The word McLuhan used to describe the transformed social totality resulting from new technologies was "environment." Our attention eventually grows numb by the pervasive atmosphere of these environments, so McLuhan described anything that supplies the means to perceive them as "anti-environment." He originally was thinking of art, and its role as a mirror to society, but it could also apply to what is known as a challenger, or disruptive, brand. Such brands act as anti-environmental change to previously established brand environments. One anti-environment example is Airbnb, whose appearance reconfigured the existing hotel market.

In the early stages of developing a brand, it is common to analyze a product or service's strengths, weaknesses, opportunities, and threats, collectively called the SWOT analysis. This is a powerful tool for understanding a brand's position in the marketplace. But how does one understand a brand's effect on culture?

This is where McLuhan's tetrad of effects may be useful. The tetrad begins by arranging four diamonds in an X, with the name of the object being studied placed in the center. Then, the process places four questions in each of the diamonds:

Upper left: What does it enhance?
Lower right: What does it obsolesce?
Lower left: What does it retrieve that had been obsolesced earlier?
Upper right: What does it reverse into when pushed to the limits of its potential?

If we applied the tetrad to any smartphone we might see that it:

Upper left: Enhances internet accessibility and convenience and aids in memory.
Lower right: Makes an ever growing number of things obsolete:
    older phones, maps, tickets, video recording equipment, etc.
Lower left: Retrieves the camera and written communication (texting).
Upper right: May (ironically) reverse interpersonal communication.

This brief analysis of the smartphone begins to define its role within the societal play of environment/anti-environment and may reveal future possibilities for either the device or something in response to the device. Because brands have both market and cultural impact, it seems logical to look at them in both lights, with the widest range of analytical tools available. In this case, McLuhan's work has much to offer.

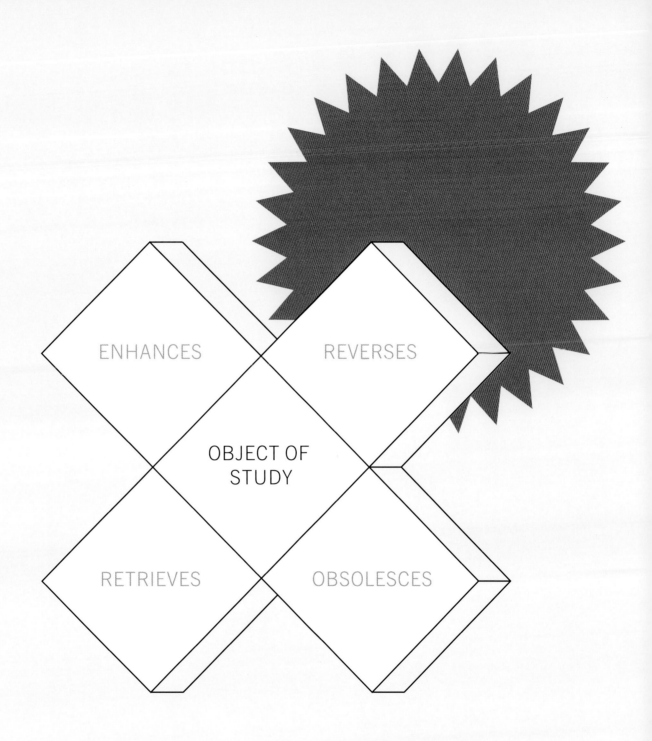

ENHANCES

REVERSES

OBJECT OF
STUDY

RETRIEVES

OBSOLESCES

Marshall McLuhan's tetrad of media effects.

33 EROTICS OF BRANDS

The benefits in
diminishing the
importance of a brand's
logical argument.

When presenting, work agencies frequently feel the compulsion to explain the work, to find relevance, and perhaps to place things in culture. (The fancy word for a logical process of interpretation is "hermeneutics.") Logic seems to be the way to make creative work digestible for clients—and ultimately worth paying for. All connections must be made and all accounts rectified.

But what does that do for the creative effort that supposedly went into the creative work? Is it allowed to exist, and connect, on a purely aesthetic, sensual level?

Susan Sontag's 1961 essay "Against Interpretation" ends with one of the most famous sentences in her oeuvre: "In place of a hermeneutics we need an erotics of art." Intriguing, but what does she mean by "erotics," and how does this apply to branding?

If we look at the origin of the word "erotics" as coming from Eros—the Greek god of passion and fertility—then the association shifts from the sexual to the creative—to life. And then for a brand to allow space for an erotics would be to create something like Restoration Hardware's Manhattan flagship—a 90,000-square-foot (8,361-square-meter) space across six floors—which is arranged so anyone can go in and just be.

Anyone is welcome to use the furniture, move through the space, and see what it's like to live the Restoration Hardware existence. Need a meeting space? Go to Restoration Hardware. A quiet place to finish your presentation? Restoration Hardware.

The level of permission is, at first, a bit unsettling; but once acclimated, it is groundbreaking. Here is a brand that created a space and then stepped back to see what happens. The goal was to allow people to make their own associations and to come to their own conclusions. Restoration Hardware made a conscious decision to truly observe and listen to people, whether they were customers or not.

Too often, product trials and customer endorsements are filtered through the tastes and restrictions of brand managers for them to have a transformative effect. But stepping back and observing how real people engage with the brand—without judgments and without any preconceived requirements—is to allow for unexpected creativity and life—in other words, a brand erotics.

Restoration Hardware's New York City flagship allows visitors to enter, sit on the furniture, and just be.

A brand's users come in a wide variety of shapes and abilities.

Much of our creative efforts are directed toward an ideal. We imagine an ideal user in an ideal situation emerging into an ideal outcome. And these ideal constructs are built upon an idealized history of previous events, events that have been fit into a narrative that is the foundation for an ideal case study. This process is then reframed as "normal."

But the ideal is not normal. "Normal" is a statistical average that applies to the largest section of the population. Normal is a convenience.

Many brands are built around convenience: the conveniences of immediacy, lower prices, or selection. And those conveniences are generally targeted for abstract, ideal audiences acting within the range of "normal."

There is always a tension between the ideal and reality. And there's nothing more real to our lived experience than our bodies. At some point in life, our bodies no longer conform to the statistically normal. If not congenital or present at birth, we all eventually diminish by disease and aging—a reality that was pointedly brought to the forefront with COVID.

There is a growing conversation about accessibility for those outside the statistically normal. In 1979 designer Patricia Moore began a three-year experiment where she simulated the changes associated with aging through clothing and devices. She was then able to respond to people, products, and environments as an elder. While still a student, Deborah Adler responded to her grandmother accidentally taking her grandfather's prescription by designing the easy-to-open, clearly labeled, color-coded ClearRX Medication System. And the product designer and ergonomics/biomechanics specialist Dan Formosa has a popular online video series where he evaluates kitchen devices by rubbing cooking oil on his hands to simulate a less-dexterous user.

Disciplines like user experience (UX) design or architecture constantly ensure their work is as accessible as possible to the widest ranges of individual mobility, perception, and cognitive abilities. UX follows the World Wide Web Consortium's Web Content Accessibility Guidelines, and architecture is regulated by local governmental standards, like the Americans with Disabilities Act (ADA). While both undergo constant review and updating, they cover only the bare minimum requirements for accessibility. And banks continue to reduce costs by closing teller windows in favor of ATMs, which creates barriers to banking to anyone who might have Parkinson's or any other limitation.

As a society, we are only beginning to fully appreciate the neurological, physical, and cognitive diversity that exists alongside the more visible ethnic and sexual diversities. This all cumulates into another opportunity for brands to establish stronger, more empathetic connections with their audience. But it requires brands to prioritize sustained relationships and to accommodate the reality of how people truly live in their bodies and in time.

Dr. Dan Formosa evaluates kitchen devices and offers design adjustments in his online video series.

Brands do not exist without an audience or users.

In the mid-1980s Robert G. Allen published his first book, *Nothing Down: How to Buy Real Estate with Little or No Money Down*. The story of how he took a U.S. $1,000 college-graduation gift and turned it into his first million within a few years was wildly compelling and launched a whole new category of seminars, workshops, and late-night television infomercials. The genre became so overinvested that it became the subject of easy parody and, while still full of potential, ceased being the topic-du-jour.

Today it seems that "branding," as a vaguely defined concept, is the new "no money down." When Kim Kardashian repeatedly speaks about "my brand," that idea has reached full saturation in the collective consciousness. And in a sense, it seems perfect for this moment in time. The ability to track public perception of brands has never been easier or more accessible, as is the ability for the public to affect brands in response. With social media, online reviews, and the ability for everyone to host their own programming on YouTube, the audience has never had more power. Every single action of a brand ripples across a series of intended and unintended consequences.

In a sense, everyone does work in branding, whether intentionally or not. And brands attempt to measure this "output" through a wide variety of research and tracking.

One of the foremost metrics is the Net Promoter Score or NPS. Developed by business strategist Fred Reichheld in 2001 (now owned by Bain & Company), the NPS asks two questions. First "How likely are you to recommend [company] to a friend or colleague?" is scored against an eleven-point scale (0–10). And the second is, "Why?" The percentage of detractors is subtracted from the promoters for the final score, with responses to "Why?" added for detail.

NPS has become a major metric in measuring brand performance. Everything can have a Net Promoter Score, including Kim Kardashian. Granted, its aggregated nature has drawbacks, but its wide acceptance as an economic/business indicator continues to make NPS a significant measure of brand health and performance.

The one limitation of the Net Promoter Score is how it's tied to transactions: would one recommend that someone else purchase or sign up for the brand. Given that brands are associations built over time, NPS seems too limited in how it reflects a relationship that is much more complex and contradictory than a brief transaction.

If everyone works in branding, then brands should consider viewing that relationship in a much more nuanced way. Because, ultimately, the audience is a full and equal partner in a brand's success.

A wax figure of American television personality, Kim Kardashian,
at Madame Tussauds London.

Not all brand extensions
are worth pursuing.

According to Google's Ngram Viewer, the slang term "flexing" (i.e. ,"to show off") has almost doubled in usage over the past couple decades. Perhaps it's a condition of social media, the growth of communications technology, or maybe even people's lack of self-confidence, but there seems to be a collective acceptance of ostentatiousness. Billionaires build their own fleets of vehicles and launch themselves into space; pickup trucks and four-wheel-drives get bigger with each year; and red carpet events are now television shows in themselves.

When brands flex, the outsized nature of the flex grates against associations that they have spent so much time and effort in building. Determining this is more a matter of degree. Something like the Spanish luxury fashion house Balenciaga's collaboration with the American footwear company Crocs is a one-time stunt that solidifies each company's respective position on the luxury/casual spectrum.

The list of misguided brand extensions is large enough to have launched a thousand online think pieces, and even a traveling exhibition known as the Museum of Failure. There are many humorous examples, like Zippo's perfume for women; Harley-Davidson's perfume, wine coolers, and ties; or Colgate's Beef Lasagna. None of these brand extensions seemed logical to the average person, and they all reached way beyond expectations, with various degrees of hubris.

These examples combine into a sliding scale of misfires and implosions. But those are mild case studies that don't reveal the pitfalls of a word, "flex," which has become so anodyne that we no longer truly hear it.

Probably the best example of flexes eroding the master brand is Donald Trump's multiple attempts to leverage his name. Part of the problem is that the brand was never really built upon well-articulated values other than a generic luxury. And the other issue is that his company, the Trump Organization, was built with financial leverage. Besides much braggadocio, little within the Trump brand was actually owned by the company.

When such is the case, one might find themselves always one step ahead of creditors and bankruptcy. And then one is perhaps too willing to license anything, which is why, besides all the real estate properties licensing the name, there has been Trump Steaks, Airline, Vodka, Ice (bottled water), Chocolate, Model Management, Shuttle, and University—to name only a few. Each one was a brand flex (to be frank) intended as a temporary stopgap until the next crisis. Astoundingly, it did work for decades, but it couldn't last forever—except as an object lesson in the pitfalls of the flex.

Note:
See 9. Blurring, 66. Permission.

Spanish fashion house, Balenciaga's, collaboration with the
American footwear company, Crocs, resulted in products like
this boot.

37 FRAMEWORKS

Strategic brand
frameworks have
limitations.

Brand strategists parse and build the world with frameworks. These mental structures expedite the analysis of markets and organizations and offer beginning steps in defining or managing a brand's essence for its audience and employees.

When organizing data, a useful framework offers a set of comparative criteria, which can lead to actionable insights. But these insights are never neutral. The intentions and needs of the users are always expressed in the framework's criteria, which, in turn, colors the final insights. Ultimately those colored insights inform subsequent actions. The biases of the analysis are expressed in the resulting actions.

A common step in brand building is the development of values. Stakeholder input (both internal and external) is synthesized into an expression of what the brand stands for, often resulting in some variation of a diagram. These diagrams come in a wide variety, ranging from pyramids, pillars, onion layers, grids, keys, and even crabs. And those diagrams come with an equally wide variety of tastes. Does the brand have five pillars or four? Does the pyramid have three layers or six? Should it be a four-square or a nine-square grid? Again, the biases of the creators are expressed in the results.

And if not a diagram, the framework might be a verbal phrase: a motto, a reminder, a platitude.

Once the framework has been agreed upon, it is used to manage day-to-day operations, evaluate employees, and guide future decisions. When applied thoughtlessly, the framework has the dangerous potential of becoming an inflexible standard.

In all cases, brand frameworks manifest utopian thinking. They are utopian wishes made into utopian form. They are always a critique of an existing state, aspiring to resolve a current situation in a future realization.

And because these brand utopias, and the frameworks upon which they are built, are the products of biased decisions, there will always be a divisive element present. It is convenient, if not politically expeditious, to get client buy-in with utopian visions and promises. But actions continue to reverberate in ways that may not have been originally intended. There will always be those who are included and those who are excluded, regardless of the initial intention.

Now that brands are finding themselves increasingly drawn into larger cultural dialogs—and increasingly using those moments to virtue-signal their position— the tried-and-true frameworks that built the profession are due for serious reevaluation. The rigidity of pillars, pyramids, grids, and mottos has to consider, and adapt to, the needs of people alongside traditional operational effectiveness. The political treacherousness of the place where brands meet people requires it.

One well-known expression of utopian thinking from the 1960s,
adapted to a typical pyramid framework.

Brand associations are built from the cultural vocabulary of preexisting symbols, signs, and conventions. But brands also have an active semantic role. They contribute to how we construct meaning, often by defining what are known as semantic domains.

A semantic domain is a specific shared set of meanings within a given context but with differences in particular details. The linguistic anthropologist Harriet Ottenheimer defines semantic domain as a "specific area of cultural emphasis." Examples include the familial (father, mother, child), body-oriented (head, shoulders, waist, feet), or social (CEO, vice president, director, assistant). Each word within a domain is learned in relation to each other to the point where some linguists propose that semantic domains may shape categories of thought.

Benjamin Lee Whorf was first to theorize a linguistic relativity, proposing that populations that don't have separate words for green and blue perceive sharper color transitions than those who do. To such groups, lime green and sky blue are basically the same color.

Semantic domains can help build connections between brands and consumers. For example, it is no accident that, when describing different shapes of wine bottles, we can point to the bottle's neck, shoulder, and foot. This frames the product as something we can approach, live with, and consume. It is now connected to our physicality and is relatable.

The introduction of categories like "sport" within brands can set a range of material, usage, and behavior expectations. Sports cars will have a certain shape and performance parameters, and sports clothing will have its own expression in fabrics and style. The semantic domain of, say, Mercedes-Benz is associated with engineering and performance, which is then articulated into different models (SUV, coupe, electric vehicle, sedans)—all of which are framed by Mercedes-Benz brand principles.

But language, and the language of brands, is more than a sequence of parts adding up to an $A + B = C$ equation of meaning. Brands can also frame a fuzzier, more poetic function. Their semantic domains can combine to generate new and sometimes astonishing ways to frame the world. For example, a shopping cart full of produce and nonprocessed food can now be called a TikTok shopping cart because of all the TikTok content on healthy eating. Of course, the person describing such a cart may recognize that difference because they usually purchase preprocessed food.

Aside from being an analytical lens, brands' semantic domains also offer possible ways in which to develop new brands. Conforming to or adopting how another brand frames something may help in the development of something as small as a new product, or it could address much larger issues like fractured politics or climate change.

The semantic domain of Starbucks eschews small, medium, and large for tall, grande, and venti.

Brands also divide people.

To decide upon an action is to divide. One path is chosen over another, eventually joining with a group of actions that are all designed to reach a goal. There isn't necessarily an ethical value applied to this decision. It is merely a matter of efficiency and maximizing one's time and effort.

Similar choices are made at every step of brand development. One must direct their efforts to a well-defined audience with a well-designed program of offerings in order to distinguish themselves from other brands—a process known as customer segmentation. And those segments can be thinly sliced according to need or intent: from the psychological to the technological to needs and values to the audience's location and so on.

The general conversation about brands speaks about how they gather the like-minded into an inclusive community. While a lofty goal, it doesn't fully consider how brands can also divide people.

When brand is seen as an aspect of marketing, this divisive aspect drives market expansion and is useful. The competition between Toyota and Nissan, Kellogg's and Nabisco, or Levi's and Wrangler, for example, finds outlets in product innovation (internally) and in almost tribal affiliations within customer segments.

But when we expand the definition of brand—an internal association from which an emotional connection is established—its divisive aspect can become problematic. Yes, trucks, biscuits, and blue jeans are all brands. But so are religions, political parties, and social movements. Even the Islamic State (ISIS) is a brand. And, as the past few years have shown, those larger brand associations have the potential to polarize the most extreme points of view.

As brands now feel pressured to take stands on cultural or political topics once considered to be outside their purview, the degree of difficulty in avoiding a misstep increases. The widespread adoption of Toyota trucks by various extremist groups like ISIS or the Taliban forced Toyota in 2022 to include a clause in sales contracts that any new Land Cruiser could not be resold within a year. This was done to prevent any potential violations of foreign exchange laws around the globe—and to keep their products out of any propaganda videos.

This all reveals that brands are not, and cannot, be neutral. A brand may enter the market with a stated strategic position, but world events often determine how that brand gathers or divides its audience and how that brand is viewed in the market and in culture.

A Toyota vehicle with Palestinian fighters on their way to military exercises in the southern Gaza Strip, December 2021.

40 GENEROSITY (AND HUMILITY)

Can a brand be seen as a gift?

The practice of branding is often seen as an extension of design. The visual is a major mode of expression in our society, so the focus often falls on new logos, celebrity spokesmodels, and innovations in product design. But this overlooks the highly collaborative aspect of branding.

Even at its most reductive, a brand requires more than one person to exist. One cannot manufacture a product and simultaneously have a brand association with the product. Like language, brands are a process of signification and interpretation. They are, in effect, a social dialogue.

If one intends to work in the branding profession, it may be beneficial to see the users' and audiences' humanity as almost an artistic medium, like paper or canvas, rather than as a resource to be exploited. This aligns with the famed American economist Irving Fisher, who wrote, "A stock of wealth existing at an instant of time is called capital. A flow of services through a period of time is called income." In this view, humanity is both a social medium and an economic one. One where the flow and exchange of services tie the whole arrangement together.

Students who aspire to enter the branding profession frequently tie it in with developing a luxury fashion brand. Given media attention on the successes of celebrity lines by the likes of Serena Williams, Rihanna, or Beyoncé, one shouldn't be surprised. This seems to align with Fisher's definition of capital: luxury lines for affluent audiences whose products amplify, display, and exchange value, which is the main lesson taught in our current era of massive income inequality.

This is not an argument for total altruism but at least a plea to begin with a degree of generosity. Even the designer working alone can practice generosity by thinking of their work as a gift to someone they have not yet met. It could be the gift of usability, affordability, accessibility, humor, or even plain beauty. The gift then becomes a means of connection.

The goal of branding is to establish a rapport with the audience. In order for that to happen, there has to be some humility, which begins with listening and leads to trust. Organizations who track the most trusted brands constantly point to companies who know their consumers well and meet them with what they need—a reputation that is becoming increasingly rare in a growing number of transactional brands.

Brands do not exist in a vacuum. They need an audience willing to pay attention and be open to the brand's proposition. And the best way to design that relationship is to begin with a generous spirit.

Note:
See 79. Skepticism.

In 1990 Smart Design partnered with OXO International to develop
the influential OXO Good Grips line, which introduced the concept
of Universal Design to mass retail, and created consumer demand
for better-performing, easier-to-use kitchen tools.

41 GO OUTSIDE YOUR LANE

The most innovative branding practitioners are the least specialized.

Maybe because it is so young—just a few decades old—that branding still has a bit of a "wild west" quality. In other words, it's too early for practices and methods to have become standardized or, rather, ossified and stale. New behaviors and frameworks are constantly entering a landscape that is constantly adapting to new political, economic, and cultural realities. New opportunities—for practitioners, brands, and audiences—reveal themselves every day. The clay is still wet.

To contrast, larger branding firms—ones usually under the control of publicly traded holding companies—tend to stick with a limited palette of offerings. This establishes reputation over time, which, in turn, allows for a more efficient profitability. In such a culture, it is common to read about firms' proprietary practices or exclusive offerings; and there is a tacit agreement as to what constitutes professional behavior.

When searching for innovation in branding, one looks to smaller, independent firms. They are not beholden to imposed profit-and-loss lines, have more flexibility in hiring, and respond to cultural change with more agility.

Independent firms tend to have more latitude in defining or reinventing their process, which allows their team members to "swim outside their lane." Borders are opened out of necessity rather than prescription.

One common interdisciplinary overlap is when designers work in brand strategy. With enough practical experience over time, and a sharp intellect, there's nothing to say that a designer can't make a valuable contribution. But it tends to be more problematic when a strategist or client manager makes a suggestion to the design team. Perhaps it is because design requires a more specific training in order to work at a high level. The training and development of a designer inculcates them into a subculture built on taste and judgment, which can easily separate them from other disciplines. And the way in which designers recognize each other through award shows and press creates a certain pride that silos disciplines and is detrimental to collegial openness.

As an alternative to taste, why not develop an appetite? Taste is restrictive while appetite is inclusive. It is a constant struggle to remain open-minded and open in process. But discovery and growth occur at the outer edges of disciplines.

Branding firms may be rewarded by specializing in highly targeted audiences. But such specialization isn't always reflected in how they build their teams. Still, there are examples of branding firms that offer services in semiotics or any other "fringe" disciplines. And this indicates the potential for the branding profession overall. A potential for interdisciplinary appetites instead of silos separated by taste and a misguided sense of professionalism.

Innovation comes from blurring professional categories and developing new fields of practice.

42 HAPTICS

The physical qualities of a designed object affect how we perceive the corresponding brand.

Interaction through touch is known as haptics. And it is an often overlooked, or neglected, channel during the design process. This is because the visual is often more likely to be given primacy over the haptic. A thicker, heavier pen may feel more substantial than ones freely available at the local bank, but it uses more material, uses more fuel in shipping, and takes up more space than its logo-festooned cheaper counterpart. The visual, usually in the form of a logo, works faster than the haptic and is usually less expensive.

Still, physical stimuli continually speaks to us, both directly through our neurology and indirectly through lived experience and memory.

The skin is the largest organ in the body, the largest sensory receptor, and the point where we begin to comprehend the world. It is more than a simple input channel; recent research indicates that neurons in the skin perform preliminary calculations about the geometry of what we touch—a quality previously thought to be exclusive to the brain.

For example, when watching a superhero movie, there is often an unsettling quality about how the characters move about—especially if their characters fly. One fires an energy bolt (without recoil), which hits another who then bounces (lightly) off a building. The problem in such cases is that filmmakers have not yet figured out how to accurately and efficiently program mass and gravity into computer-generated footage. And without that sense of weight and momentum it becomes difficult to imagine being Spiderman. The sense of physical being remains out of reach because we inherently know what it feels like to move through space, bounce off surfaces, and live in a world governed by Newtonian physics.

Haptic information communicates mass, weight, and momentum in a way that verbal and visual methods can only symbolize. Physical brands have a unique opportunity to convey "authenticity" by attending to even the smallest detail: the crispness of a corner on a folding carton, a secure click on a garment closure, or the depth of a punt on the bottom of a wine bottle. This is where the progression of brands into the digital realm lags behind the physical. Which is quicker and safer? Reaching over to turn a dashboard knob while driving, or diverting your attention to a screen in order to change a radio station? Human nature may prefer to focus on the new and technological, but so much remains to be gained by paying attention to the haptic.

Jean-Baptiste Carpeaux's sculpture, *Ugolino and His Sons*, depicts
the effect of fingers pressing into flesh; an effect famously attributed
to Michelangelo.

Moments of verbal interaction are a growing opportunity for brand interaction.

If you say, "Hey Siri, beam me up, Scotty," into an Apple device, Siri responds with, "We're having a wee bit of trouble." And if you ask what Siri thinks of Google Assistant, the response is, "I'm a big fan of good listeners and helpful beings." This begins to describe the blurry area where brands overlap.

Up until now, brands have relied on visual systems to distinguish themselves. And the introduction of digital assistants hints at a future where brands speak with their own voice and personality. Today you can ask Siri to place your regular Starbucks order, but Siri will soon be replaced by a more brand-specific entity.

One can easily imagine voice-based assistants with distinctive accents and ways of speaking. If brands have personalities, then this is the next step toward a more dimensional character and a specifically defined audience. Linguistic flourishes like Cockney rhyming slang, French Verlan, or even pig Latin could express a brand's spirit. And generational references, driven by user data, could expedite interactions and increase customer satisfaction.

How amazing would it be for a digital assistant to say, "Doh!" instead of, "I'm sorry…"? Wouldn't that feel like it was made by a real person?

How often have we heard lines like, "They really speak to me?" Now, a brand really can—but only to a point.

The first hurdle to this sort of verbal interaction is the usual corporate fear of wanting to be distinctive but not too distinctive. Personas would be judged against a nondescript set of criteria like, "Is it clear, simple, and direct?" And personality quirks need to balance individuality with the possibility that it would stand out too much and inhibit efficiency.

The second hurdle is the gatekeepers of the device and operating system's developers. For example, Apple is famous for requiring third-party developers to conform to Apple standards of content and behavior in its app store. Any brand-specific assistant would be measured against both community and developer standards. Additionally the wild card of permissions is also controlled by the developer. Chances are that the brand's assistant would not be available unless it was turned on in settings. And the design and management of those filters are outside the brand's influence.

In other words, users would still need to ask Siri for permission to speak with Starbucks.

These sorts of controls shouldn't be seen as a limit but rather as creative stimulus. Brands are already bleeding across the digital space of verbal communication— like they already do in real-life person-to-person interactions. The only limitation is our imagination.

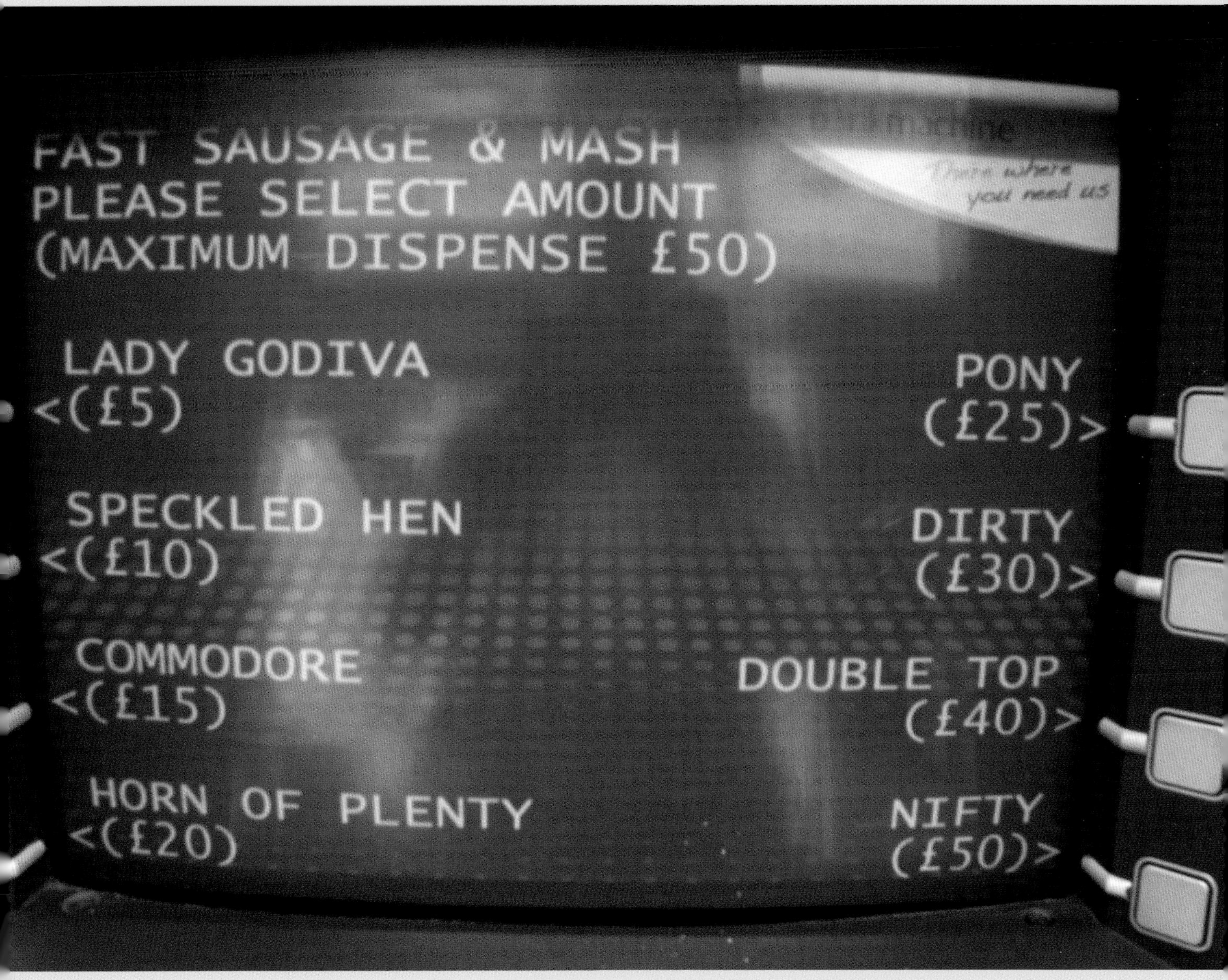

FAST SAUSAGE & MASH
PLEASE SELECT AMOUNT
(MAXIMUM DISPENSE £50)

LADY GODIVA
<(£5)

PONY
(£25)>

SPECKLED HEN
<(£10)

DIRTY
(£30)>

COMMODORE
<(£15)

DOUBLE TOP
(£40)>

HORN OF PLENTY
<(£20)

NIFTY
(£50)>

Certain cash points in east London allow users to select Cockney
Rhyming Slang as the language of choice.

HETEROGENEITY

Data is an incomplete way of understanding a brand's audience.

As brands become more driven and directed by the collection and analysis of data, it helps to be reminded of its nature. Data does not exist on its own. We make it. And truth, whatever that is, does not emanate from data objectively.

One of the constant forces in data, which always has to be rationalized to some degree, is heterogeneity across different studies. This is the inconsistency of results, not due to chance, which may stem from varying clinical approaches in the design of the study or the settings used; or there may be statistical differences between studies. The reasons why one would want to combine studies, known as a meta analysis, is to improve overall precision; increase the generalizability of individual study results; answer questions not posed in the individual studies; settle differences between studies; or, importantly, to generate new hypotheses.

Results from a meta analysis seem to be better because that review outweighs individual studies, but they aren't necessarily more reliable. They capture what happened, not necessarily what is happening. And if there is excessive heterogeneity, the validity of the meta analysis is in question.

The term for "truth" in ancient Greek philosophy is "aletheia," which translates to "unconcealedness," "disclosure," or "revealing." This definition was later adopted by the German philosopher Martin Heidegger as an uncommon way to think about truth. To Heidegger, truth was like sunlight breaking through a clearing in the forest. As one walks from clearing to clearing, each bright spot is true to itself. So all data does is reveal a moment.

Placing the role of data in this light puts appropriate limits on its veracity and role as a tool. Data is not the wellspring of objective truth. As long as we measure the world with tools (even slightly) deformed by human intention, the role for the individual remains.

Heterogeneity becomes an asset to be encouraged instead of resolved. When branding teams are homogeneous, they tend to fall into groupthink, which causes them to overrate their decision-making capabilities and to blind them to collective weaknesses.

The use of the term "heterogeneity" instead of "diversity" is intentional. In this case, heterogeneity describes a collective that purposely integrates different people, while diversity implies divergence from the homogeneous. The goal is an active engagement of individuals stress testing and improving each other's contribution with the hopes that the results will connect across a range of audiences. Each with their own individual statistical profiles.

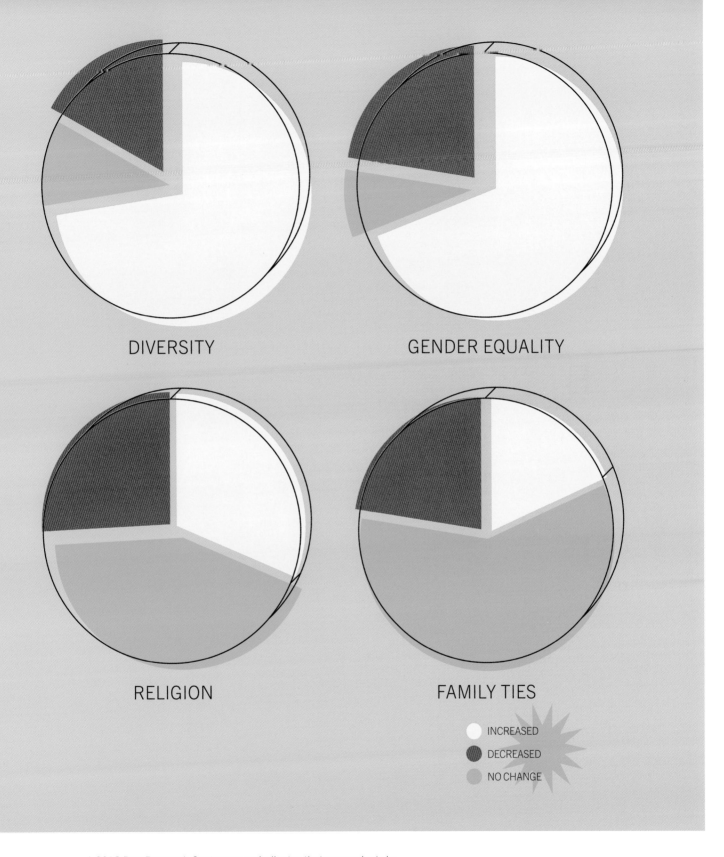

DIVERSITY

GENDER EQUALITY

RELIGION

FAMILY TIES

INCREASED

DECREASED

NO CHANGE

A 2018 Pew Research Center survey indicates that respondents in twenty-seven countries think that diversity and gender equality have increased, while connections to religion and family ties have diminished.

Remember that brands exist in time.

The invention of movable type, the lightbulb, or the internet introduced such sudden and profound changes to human existence that we wonder how anyone lived and worked beforehand. It is almost as if they sprang forth from their inventors' minds fully formed and perfect. Stories like the one of Samuel F. B. Morse, the inventor of the telegraph, transmitting the device's first message—"What hath God wrought?"—only contribute to the misperception of innovation.

The wondrous, magical springing forth of innovation and invention is a myth. In actuality, innovation is the genealogical result of many precedents coming together in a historical, material, technological, cultural, economical, and political moment. Innovation and invention, like brands, are reflections of their moment in time. They are responses to the past and present. And, contrary to current commentary, designers and innovators do not "make" the future. Rather they work in the present—a present constantly bumping into the future.

It is easier to describe isolated slices of time than the vectors moving through time. And our conclusions about what happened, what is happening, or what will happen are often based on insufficient information.

Under this construct, we can see a brand as a temporal meeting point. And since all objects and conditions are always becoming something else—either through growth or entropy—brands are never fixed. They may be in the present, but that present is tumbling through time.

Keeping temporality in mind serves, in a way, as a pressure release. The mindset of many designers is to strive for a platonic ideal—done once, perfectly, and never to be altered. Creative work is in constant dialogue with work that came before and, thus, is an ongoing critique of the past, informed by the siren song of an idealized future, then deformed by individual taste and pride.

An appreciation of how the past flows through the lens of the present can help check one's ego and deflate the breathless bullshit of "futureproofing." Developing a brand isn't the creation of a perfect state through an engineered process but the recruitment of multiple energies that are then focused into a mutual agreement. And the future is rarely what we imagined it could be. What rational person in the Cold War era could have imagined Mikhail Gorbachev, the last leader of the Soviet Union, appearing in a Pizza Hut commercial? Perhaps what that suggests is that futureproofing is either an insistence for continued momentum or resistance to change.

The first McDonald's in Moscow opened in 1990, a year before the dissolution of the Soviet Union.

Pay attention to how
a brand "sounds" to
the ear.

Attention to how sounds, names, or phrases hit the ear can make brand messaging more melodious. But not all sounds sing to every ear. It also helps to keep neurodivergent groups in mind. For example, misophonia, or selective sound sensitivity syndrome, is a disorder in which certain sounds trigger uncomfortable emotional or physiological responses. Frequent triggers are oral sounds, like chewing or repetitive tapping.

Marshall McLuhan once said, "Visual space is the space of detachment; acoustic space is tactile. It is the space of involvement." We often see things through language—the caption, if you will. But sound and tone tell us if we're near or far, in a big room, or in an intimate one. The auditory situates us physically and emotionally. And a good example of the tactility that McLuhan refers to can be found in ASMR.

Autonomous Sensory Meridian Response (ASMR) is a tingling sensation along the scalp, neck, and upper spine commonly triggered by stimuli that ranges from the auditory, visual, haptic, environmental, or narrative. The version that has recently drawn large audiences on social media is auditory ASMR. In that form, a person on camera makes soft, frictive sounds into a binaural microphone—from whispering, to tapping, scraping, rubbing, or crumpling. The effect is maximized when listening through headphones for proper stereo sound.

There seems to be high demand for soothing, relaxing sound therapy in this stressful world. One of the more popular YouTube channels, *Gentle Whispering ASMR,* has over 2 million subscribers.

The physical response to ASMR shows there is a neurological response to how things are said. Besides the text of a message, there is the energy of expression, something of great importance when naming a brand but rarely addressed in any verbal guidelines document.

Naming teams often benefit from having someone with linguistics training on board. They can advise if a word is easily spoken in a variety of languages, and they can help focus upon the energetics of phonemes. Probably the best-known example of would be "Kodak," which George Eastman created because, as he said, "The letter K had been a favorite with me—it seemed a strong, incisive sort of letter." It also bears an onomatopoeic resemblance to the click of a camera shutter.

Whenever an orchestra or band gathers to rehearse, much time is spent on the attack and energy of individual notes, which corresponds to the attention linguists give to phonemes. These building blocks of communication carry as much emotional information as the content of the text. The vector and valence of a brand's language may not be the easiest thing to agree upon, but it does deserve discussion.

Autonomous sensory meridian response (ASMR) is a tingling
sensation commonly triggered by specific auditory stimuli, like soft
fricative sounds created by whispering, scratching, or rubbing.

47 IDENTITY

Brands play a major role in our personal identities.

As we collectively make brand associations in our minds, brands, in return, have an equally significant role in creating us. The clothes we wear, the music we prefer, the objects in our homes, the organizations to which we belong, and the schools we attend are all selected as an expression of how we see ourselves in the world. They represent us, and they make us.

Our identity is built with brands. And, consequently, this identity affects how others perceive us in return. We make different assumptions about people whether they collect manga figurines, sports memorabilia, or bongs.

The question then arises: Is our personal identity directly connected to our authentic selves? In other words, is our identity a thing or a collage of things? Over time, our experience grows, our tastes change, and our thoughts about brands shift as we interact with them. Given the constant flux of the market, our identity, too, is equally in flux. Our identity becomes a collage of fluctuating brand associations.

This idea evokes the most famous line from French author Simone de Beauvoir's 1949 book, *The Second Sex*, which reads, "One is not born but becomes woman." De Beauvoir wrote how in a male-dominated world, female is defined relative to male. Based on that, our identity is built in relation to, and defined by, a brand-saturated world.

Now let's extend the theme to the identities of brands themselves. Graphic design is a collage practice. Designers collage preexisting letter forms and writing systems, typefaces, colors, images, and layout motifs, together into a visual identity system. Copywriters collage existing words, grammar, and common phrases into a verbal system. UX designers work with preexisting behaviors, or routines, and generally accepted navigational conventions. And brand strategists look to business case studies, cultural trends, and competitors when building a positioning. Brand identities themselves are collages.

If all identity, both personal and brand, is made up of changing elements existing in a shifting universe, then authenticity is a situational agreement. This changes the role of anyone responsible for "building a brand"—an overused and egotistical term. Brands do not spring forth fully formed from the creator's mind. Brands are not built. They are corralled; they are directed; they are brought into the world. And perhaps this is done not by a brand engineer but by a brand doula.

The doula is a trained companion who supports a client in giving birth. They are sensitive to the environment, the people present, and the energy and movement as things progress. And it is that egoless sensitivity to the moment that is called for in both the branding profession and life in general.

Note:
Designer and strategist Rudi Petry first suggested the metaphor of brand doula during a class discussion in the School of Visual Arts Masters in Branding program.

Before music streaming, a large record collection was a common method of self-expression. The collection became, in a sense, one's self-portrait.

Exercise caution when partnering with brand influencers.

There is probably no better indicator of the degree that social media has infected our minds than overhearing a conversation where one person expresses a desire to become an influencer (generously defined as an expert with a sizable following).

Any notable moment while scrolling the feed is ephemeral—forgotten with the next moment, and the one after that, and the one after that. The aggregate message of influencers tends to be one of general consumption instead of specific brand alignment.

On the personal level, any attempt to become an influencer—by dumping a bucket of ice over one's head, skateboarding to a pop music hit from the 1970s, or doing a quick-change video from a frumpy outfit to a revealing one all in hopes of being paid to endorse a brand—is more akin to playing the lottery than a well-considered career move.

Influencers are interchangeable pieces in a collective race to the bottom. They are subject to the constantly changing compensation policies and terms of service of the platforms they rely on; and they tend not to be as fully vetted as celebrity endorsers. This then connects any affiliated brand to the influencer's scandals, arrests, or personal tragedies. Because, as some influencers have discovered, being famous is often not the life of wine and roses they would have hoped for.

Now, brands can avoid the personal complexities associated with human influencers. Media companies are developing computer-generated influencers targeted to specific demographic and regional audiences. Recent personalities are Rozy from Korean media company Sidus Studio X, Kyra from TopSocial India, and Lil Miquela from Brud in Los Angeles.

These digital influencers will be twenty-two forever, are free of any significant health issues (unless specifically programmed), and steer clear of any dangerous controversies. Upon launch, each quickly grew audiences in the tens of thousands and signed a significant number of sponsorship agreements.

Given the sheer volume of influencers and the algorithmic landscape, the share of voice measured against return on investment makes influencers a questionable choice for brands. They are too disconnected from a brand's authentic position to be worthwhile, unless the influencer is an authentic member of the brand's audience.

One notable inclusion of influencers occurs on the social media platform Clubhouse. The app icon changes frequently to a photo of a user who "represents the Clubhouse community at its best" making a C shape with their hand. It is a way to recognize club leaders who might go unnoticed elsewhere, underscores the highest ideals of what the brand wants to be known for, and offers a mutual halo-effect, which feels inclusive instead of exploitative. The practice demonstrates how relationships with social media influencers can be more than transactional.

This portrait of Daniel Anderson and Calista Wu, two influential users on the social media platform Clubhouse, was used in a series of app icons. In each image, the subject made the letter "C" with their hand.

19 INTIMACY

Know the difference
between personalization
and an intimate
brand relationship.

In the movie *Animal House*, new members of the Delta Tau Chi fraternity are sworn in with an oath. The fraternity president says, "I (state your name) do hereby pledge allegiance to the frat with liberty and fraternity for all," and the ensemble responds, "I, state your name, do hereby pledge allegiance…." The scene pokes fun at the appearance of personalization in a nonpersonalized scenario.

We experience this same nonpersonalized personalization every single day. It is common to receive emails that address you by name or robotic phone calls that begin, "We've been trying to reach you concerning your…." In each case, these messages are the result of an algorithm working within some sort of customer relationship management platform and enhanced by a growing body of research on the psychology of decision making.

Initially customer-relationship management systems offer the benefit of efficiency. A well-integrated system removes the silos between sales, product development, and management so that all can work from the same data—whether it be operational or analytical. Then, ideally, product offerings become more responsive to customer behavior, messaging becomes better targeted, conflicts are resolved more satisfactory, and waste is reduced. The brand relationship begins to take on a sense of intimacy.

Algorithms also can add a degree of intimacy in the production or distribution process. Levi's introduced mass-customized jeans for women in the mid-1990s and has developed the offering to include pairs that have been individually laser-distressed. Converse allows customers to mix and match colors across sneaker components like tongues, soles and seams; as well as the option to add text to the shoe's sides. And streaming services like Spotify analyze the listener's history to suggest content that can continue the mood.

When done correctly, these adjustments and personalization enhance a consumer's quality of life and sense of agency. The brand sees and understands the consumer, and the consumer is able to be and act more like themself.

There is a growing body of work that uses brand intimacy as a metric to measure a brand's health or relevance. Depending on how one defines it, one can connect feelings of intimacy to a brand's market value. This seems worthwhile, since brands comprise the associations held in the consumer's mind. Ultimately, this is not true intimacy. That comes from an investment in time and attention, which, thankfully, is still the domain of people. The goal is not to confuse real intimacy with its algorithmic simulation.

Personalized Coca-Cola bottles with the names Kirsty and Barry.

If brands are about connection, then all branding professionals should avoid jargon.

For a profession that claims to be concerned with forming positive connections between people, branding doesn't do itself any favors in its use of jargon. Granted, every professional group uses certain terms out of expediency or tactically. The United States Army's "MRE" is quicker to say than "Meals Ready to Eat," and hospital announcements are sometimes coded to avoid panic. But branding folks are probably better off in aiming to speak as clearly as possible.

Such a practice of constant clarification can result in equally clear thinking and effective work. It would also prevent one from saying things like, "Let's leverage a different earcon to hit our BHAG." "Leverage" means "use." "Earcon" is a combination of "ear" and "icon," or "audio icon." "BHAG" is "big, hairy, audacious, goal."

Jargon is seductive. It unites working groups and helps signal competence to others like a secret password. But its seductiveness also contributes to groupthink and sameness.

"North Star" is a current bit of jargon that has virulently spread throughout the branding world. Whoever came up with the term is admittedly a genius. It is evocative and much more appealing than "BHAG." But now consider some poor client having to sit through a series of potential agency presentations that all talk about finding their "North Star."

The term "low-hanging fruit" was especially popular around 2005 to 2010. Meaning "an easily achievable action," it became a thing to say if one didn't have much to say. A series of proposed tactics would be presented, and someone would inevitably identify a segment as "low-hanging fruit." Everyone else would nod in agreement, the meeting would continue, and the person who said it could then suppress the creeping fear of appearing incompetent.

Eventually every bit of branding jargon begins to grate on the nerves. Perhaps it's because the profession is built upon the presentation—where one must be polished and confident to be believable. And part of that presence comes from experience and practice. But where musicians develop a "finger memory," branding should avoid a "verbal memory."

If language is a mirror of the intellect, and if the internal mental landscape of a brand's audience is in constant flux, then a rigid toolbox of language should be the last thing to be called upon.

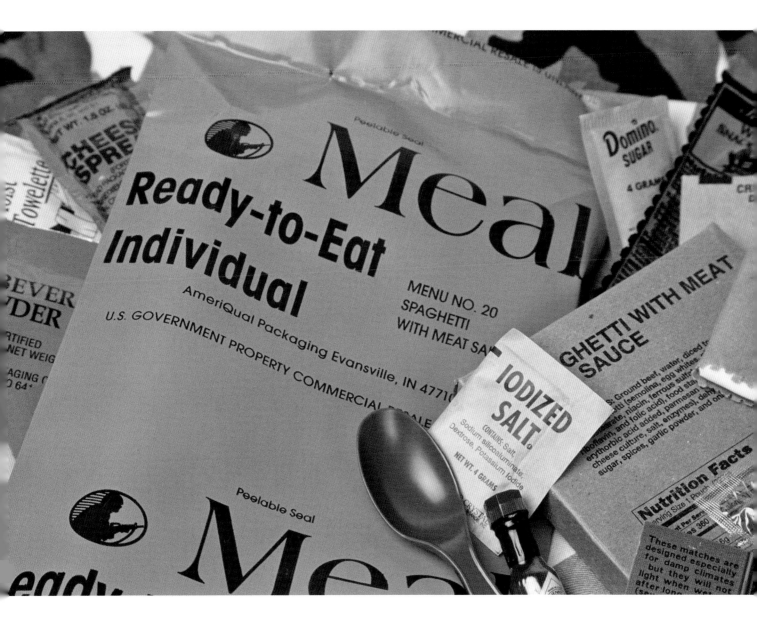

The United States Army's "Meal Ready to Eat," better known as
an "MRE."

The way in which brand archetypes are currently used is more of a crutch than a useful tool.

If one is a "creative" responsible for turning out a constant stream of work, one develops a toolkit of strategies and resources. It might include pulling inspiration from children's games, obscure packaging from Soviet-controlled East Germany, or typefaces from the 1970s. In brand development, one of the more persistent resources was inspired by Swiss psychiatrist Carl Gustav Jung's concept of the archetype.

Where common psychoanalytic theory investigates the roots of a personal unconscious, Jung believed that human behavior was also informed by a collective unconscious. This unconscious consists of elements common to all human beings—spanning regions, cultures, and time—and laddering up into models he called "archetypes."

Jung's influence found its expression in contemporary branding through the pioneering work of Carol S. Pearson, PhD. Her original six basic archetypes—Orphan, Wanderer, Warrior, Altruist, Innocent, and Magician—was intended for a general audience, especially those on personal journeys. Six years later, she expanded the list to twelve—Caregiver, Creator, Destroyer, Fool, Innocent, Lover, Magician, Orphan, Sage, Seeker, Ruler, Warrior—and placed them along the hero's journey, which is another archetype.

Pearson partnered with Margaret Mark, an advertising strategist and consumer insight practitioner, to test the archetype tool against Young & Rubicam's Brand Asset Valuator, a proprietary longitudinal study conducted over an extended period. The results aligned a different set of twelve—Caregiver, Creator, Explorer, Hero, Innocent, Jester, Lover, Magician, Outlaw, Regular Guy/Gal, Ruler, Sage—within the motivations of individuals and brands.

Since this work was published, the twelve archetype model has become a popular way to define a brand's positioning and behavior. But with frequent use, it often runs the danger of becoming a crutch, or even a gimmick, rather than the guide it was intended. As Mark and Pearson wrote, archetypes are "not the 'engine' of the brand, as is relevant differentiation, but [they] can be the force that accelerates the brand's power and increases its momentum."[1]

A didactic adherence to twelve exact archetypes is an impoverished approach. Jung and his followers realized that there were many more, and that there was flexibility in the system, as evidenced by the constant shift in Pearson's work. To insist on a set list of twelve archetypes is to limit the possibility of discovering new definitions and territories. The idea of an archetype should be an inspiration and not a checklist.

Note:
1. Margaret Mark and Carol S. Pearson. *The Hero and the Outlaw: Building Extraordinary Brands through the Power of Archetypes*. New York. McGraw-Hill, 2001.

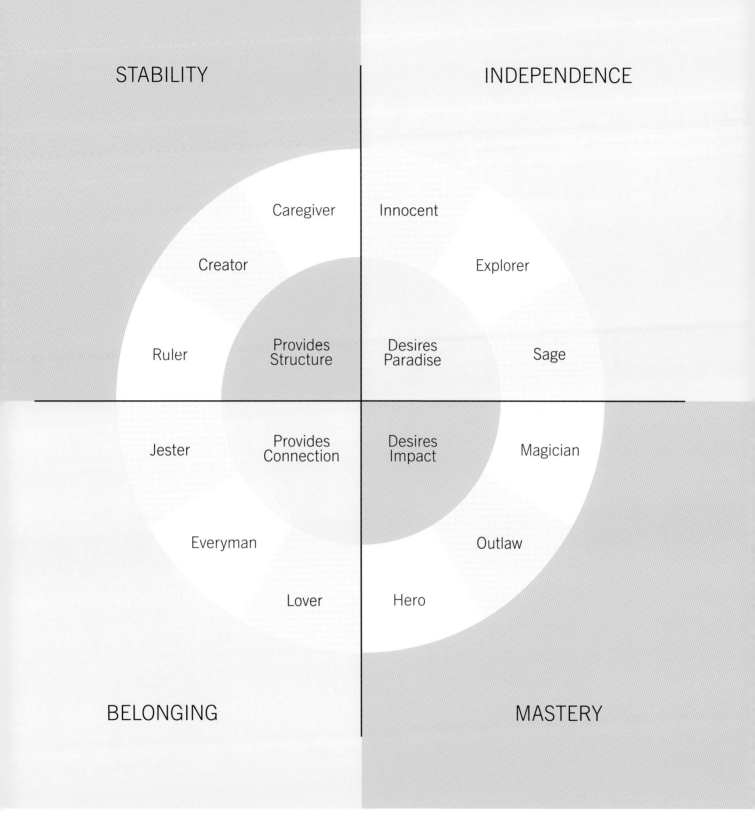

STABILITY

INDEPENDENCE

Caregiver

Innocent

Creator

Explorer

Ruler

Provides
Structure

Desires
Paradise

Sage

Jester

Provides
Connection

Desires
Impact

Magician

Everyman

Outlaw

Lover

Hero

BELONGING

MASTERY

Many brand strategists use this version of Carol Pearson and
Margaret Mark's archetype diagram.

Human beings are both the reason for the brand and a cliché in brand communication.

Presenting a brand system, an advertising campaign, or a graphic system often requires that the work be approved by a group of people. Everyone gathers around a conference table to be taken through a well-rehearsed presentation. Goals are restated, strategic insights are revealed, a series of "what-ifs" are asked, and finally the work is presented.

Afterwards, the traditional question-and-answer segment begins. Following a series of minor logistical questions, someone is bound to ask the old chestnut: "Can you include a picture of a person to make it more human?"

Besides the logical fallacy of asking humans, working for other humans in order to connect with even more humans, to make things more human, there is the commonness of such a request. Until animals gain the desire or ability to participate in human society or extraterrestrials take up residence on Earth, one can safely assume that if the work was created by a human—even with the assistance of algorithms—it is sufficiently human.

Sadly there are too many examples of this sloppy rationale. Wealth management campaigns show senior citizens playing with grandchildren or walking along a beach in blissful retirement. Pharmaceutical campaigns for erectile medication show couples side-by-side in individual bathtubs. Or community centers select logos featuring human-shaped sprites. Such imagery is so clichéd, it becomes invisible.

A request to depict humans is usually made out of anxiety. To see a smiling face, a couple enjoying a sunset, a family playing in the backyard is to work within safe parameters. Similar tropes have worked in the past, so they must work in this case.

A case can be made for such continuity. The mind uses patterns to relieve the cognitive load of continually perceiving the world. If something resembles or acts like anything else, it is quickly understood. These patterns can then act as a shorthand, which can then be affirmed, tweaked slightly, or upended, depending on the desired effect. When done on behalf of the audience, the inclusion of human imagery is thoughtful and fully intentional.

The one notable shift in recent imagery has been the representation of people from across a range of backgrounds and identities. Where once it was common to see painfully obvious collections of diversity—one from column A, another from column B, etc.—the issue of purposeful representation seems to be receiving long-overdue consideration. In such a case, this is to be celebrated. As long as it doesn't fall back into tropes of couples on the beach walking hand-in-hand. Then the opportunity for thoughtful imagery will have been wasted.

Tropes like couples on a beach are so cliched, they become virtually invisible.

The first moments with a brand can have long-lasting effects.

Much energy goes into the packaging of luxury or high-tech products. The precision of their quality-controlled production needs to survive the international shipping process. So brands spend many hours perfecting every single aspect of packaging material and construction, regardless of how small it is.

Such attention to the smallest detail signals the level of care applied across the whole brand, whether it be product design, the retail experience, customer support, or usage. Everything ladders up into how the brand is perceived and consistently exhibits the company's values. In fact, packaging can be so well-considered as to inspire a whole genre of social media posts known as "unboxing."

A theatrical first interaction/performance can act as a wonderful portal into a brand's worldview. Since this usually requires more material and time to prepare, it is often limited to the luxury sector: tissue-wrapped shoes and clothing—sealed with a sticker and placed in a turn-top, rope-handled bag, which has been printed with double hits of spot color—graciously handed over by a sales associate who has made a point to step around the counter and see the customer to the door.

While less common, there are some performative flourishes at the mass market level. Brooklinen sheets are clearly marked "short side" and "long side;" which makes putting them on the bed much more enjoyable and enhances the relaxation of that night's sleep. And housekeeping at the Strand Hotel in Los Angeles signals a clean bathroom with a whimsical sticker placed on the toilet paper roll, which depicts a pooping stick figure.

It's important to realize that the intended audience for these moments should be individuals. When it becomes a public spectacle, like the flashy light shows available on Teslas, the effect is more ego aggrandizement than one of personal attention. And when an unboxing video is the point of the brand, like the LOL Surprise Egg craze of 2018–2019, the effect is cynical consumption.

Looking at an initial interaction as an individualized performance may reveal missed opportunities. For example, there must be a better way to attach tags to clothing than horrible, small plastic filaments. And there must be a better way to call upon the next person in line than robotically asking, "May I help the next guest, please?"

Seeing such initial interactions as opportunities to build anticipation, confirm good intentions, and strengthen brand values can go far to increase loyalty and word of mouth. Beyond such tactical concerns, it becomes the basis for a sense of hospitality, something that seems to be in short supply these days.

The LOL Surprise Egg doll was only meant to be unwrapped, and for that unwrapping to appear on social media. How does that benefit the consumer?

There is no such thing
as a perfect color,
typeface, etc.

The French writer Voltaire is attributed with the saying, "Perfect is the enemy of good." In other words, looking for the perfect typeface and color is akin to believing in magic and superstition. A customer won't decide based on typographic or color details alone, nor the lighting scheme of product photography or the number of values in a brand positioning. Yes, God is in the details, but so is the Devil.

The elements of a visual identity system traditionally begin with a typographic style and a color palette. The name is set in the appropriate typeface, a complementary face (if needed) is chosen for supplementary text, and colors are selected to visually tie things together.

Before desktop publishing, a designer would have to rely on their imagination and ability to draw when choosing an appropriate typeface. A quick sketch first, an educated guess at point size and column width, and the job was sent off to the typesetter. Things were a bit easier then because there weren't so many fonts available. A designer was limited by their type house's catalog, and the burden of choice was lighter. These days, the digital revolution has brought so many typefaces to market, at varying degrees of detail and quality, that it is virtually impossible to know what is available.

One advantage that desktop publishing brought to design was the ability to enter text and then instantly see what it looks like in a variety of typefaces. Changing one element—size, weight, italic, or not—no longer took a separate call to the typesetter. It was instantaneous. A designer's selection process expanded from the envisioned and abstract to a question of feel.

A similar shift happened in color. Where once designers were limited to sketching or short production runs—silk screen, rub-down transfers—they now can change colors instantly. And with that infinite variety came the creeping anxiety of finding the perfect typeface and the perfect color palette. Designers and clients now run the danger of not being able to choose with absolute confidence, relegating them to magic and superstition.

And data makes things only worse. While product lead at Google, Marissa Mayer famously A/B tested forty-one shades to find the perfect blue for the home page— which sounds like a circle of design hell.

Perfection disappears with the momentum of continual action. The world is in constant change, and there are no stable platonic objects. Decisions should be based on how something makes connections rather than how it measures up to a mental ideal. And, given how the world is moving faster and faster, chances are that an opportunity for a better decision will arrive soon enough.

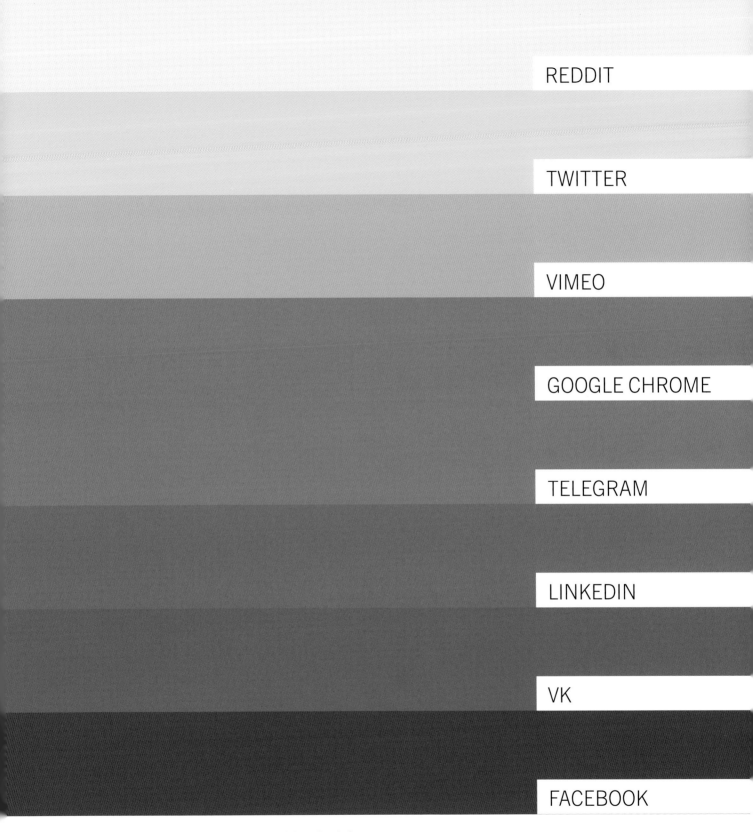

REDDIT

TWITTER

VIMEO

GOOGLE CHROME

TELEGRAM

LINKEDIN

VK

FACEBOOK

The range of blues used by eight social media platforms.

The insistence on strict
compliance to brand
standards can miss out
on larger opportunities.

During any creative endeavor, there is a tension between the project's platonic ideal and the messiness of the process. Pure and unsullied versus complex and compromised. This is the struggle of bringing something into the world.

Developing and distributing a product or service is the collected result of more than one person's work. And this merging of multiple skills and ideas requires compromise at every step. While it can be exciting to see a team of collaborators will vagueness into sharp focus, navigating different personalities and agendas can also be distracting.

Even within the most collegial group, at some point there will be a need to manage and align behaviors. How can one channel a group's energy without alienating individual parties? How to empower people so they feel pride of possession and participation? And how to then expand this to the audience? Because the audience is equally responsible for a brand's success.

When practiced badly, brand management settles for continued vigilance over asset usage and little else. Everything is compared to the brand's guidelines and judged to be on brand or off. In this mindset, if the logo doesn't appear in exactly the proper shade of red, or against the proper background color, it is rejected outright. All assets are strictly regulated.

Granted, it is important for things to be consistent. But consistency is only one step toward maintaining a brand's coherence. The audience is intelligent enough to know that an Oreo cookie with green filling, instead of white, is still an Oreo cookie. And they're intelligent enough to suspect that the green filling might be a St. Patrick's Day reference. Meaning is not created by an unwavering constellation of brand assets. It is contextual, and it is always in dialogue with other narratives.

There needs to be a larger operating frame of reference, a more generous metaphor than the corral of assets or the central command of behaviors.

Consider that brands do not create an audience. And they do not create desire in and of itself. They channel existing desires through the brand. The metaphor should be one of sailing: using and redirecting prevailing forces with an end goal in mind.

Yes, please make sure that the Oreo filling is the correct color, but also think about how the brand might connect with an audience by offering a rainbow of filling colors. In this specific instance, recognizing the LGBTQ audience can expand how people think of Oreos. The brand then moves beyond being a mere product into a different level of relevance.

Oreo cookies with differently colored fillings developed to connect
with the LGBTQ+ audience.

The relationship between brands and overriding cultural narratives.

Consumer society couldn't have developed unless the majority of people agreed upon matters of value, production, distribution, and control. And a good deal of that alignment was regulated through master narratives. These are the stories we tell ourselves, the stories we believe to be true, and the basis upon which we judge others. They run the gamut—from capitalism and open markets to the scientific method, democracy, Western civilization, religion, Manifest Destiny, the Monroe Doctrine, and Hollywood. They are, in a sense, the metaphorical glue of society.

When there were only a handful of media outlets—national television networks and news agencies—the collective narrative was more coherent, which helped align the audience into a mass market. Advertising had the dual function of selling and reinforcing the status quo, and the values and aesthetics of the dominant culture echoed throughout popular entertainment.

Technological changes in communication—such as cable television, the Internet, and social media platforms—along with the global explosion of markets, allowed different voices to reach increasingly fragmented audiences. Instead of a shared master narrative and aesthetic, public discourse(s) fractured into a multitude of historical-contextualist narratives. While truth really is an ongoing process of revealing, today's public realm cannot even agree upon that. Everyone has access to different truths, competing revelations of different histories and different contexts. "Do your own research" now describes a state where a once-agreed upon process is detached from the foundations of rigor, logic, and research.

In a situation where there is no agreement about truth, the potential exists for alienation, where people stop caring and adopt an attitude of radical apathy. This adds complexity to the roles of brands in society. Do they build upon earlier master narratives like family, displays of status, or the common good? Or do they attempt to exploit this social fragmentation?

The traditional marketing response suggests that the better targeted the brand or offering is, the more profitable each audience member becomes. On a tactical level, this seems like a good approach. But brands are more complex than that. They are how we view the world, understand each other, and navigate through life.

This then becomes an issue of ambition. If fueling enthusiasm for a brand is a common goal, then what if the tactical energy usually directed toward customer conversions was broadened so as to identify and build new master narratives? Yes, an ambitious goal. But if not us, then who? Earlier brands of church, school, and country built a world that, while not equitable, did much to unify humanity. And the opportunity continually presents itself for us to do it again—and hopefully better.

Significant historical events, like the Moon landing, can align people across
political borders; as shown by these newspaper readers in Amsterdam.

Brands don't have to
explain everything.

One of the disconnects between a brand's origin in the boardroom and the market stems from the presence of logic. The boardroom's duty to shareholders and owners includes maximizing profits while minimizing risk. And since risk measures historical behaviors and outcomes against potential deviation from the desired outcome, assessing risk is a logical process.

When business, and eventually brand, strategy is formulated, logic is part of the decision-making process. Further down the line, logic persists in how the brand is marketed. Saying that an alarm system equals safety is basic logic. This equals that thing. Or this does not equal that other thing. Even if a campaign makes a metaphorical or metonymic connection, it is still a symbolic bit of logic equating one thing to another.

The great television writer David Milch once wrote, "Logic is a limping stepchild of the true processes of the spirit. It's an illusion. It's a defective little parlor trick. Associations are the way that we perceive. Electrical connections caused by the juxtapositions of experience. That's the way we are really built."[1]

When an audience learns about a brand, it isn't always done through a logical argument. The experience is bookended between a series of unconnected moments and measured against a lifetime of lived experience. To try and control that individual process with a logical argument seems limiting, if not a fool's errand. You can't make someone love you through logic.

Logical arguments close mental loops. Things are answered and resolved. Thinking is over. But mental loops that remain open allow for sustained thought. Perhaps this is an aspect of sustained love relationships—anyone involved continues to think of the other person.

An open loop has an element of mystery. Questions are never fully answered. The narrative never ends. The relationship goes on.

A sense of mystery seems to be inherent in more successful brands. It may not be the mystery of a detective novel, but it could simply be the mystery of open potentials or open questions. An airline could be built around the question, "Where to next?" A fashion brand could be, "Who will you become?" A furniture line could be, "How sophisticated is your apartment?" Or even, "How different are you from your parents?"

Granted, it may be difficult, if not inappropriate, for a corn chip brand to have a sense of mystery. But a sustained effort to not explain every single detail of a brand may make our collective branded experience a degree more interesting.

Note:
1. HBO.com, Inside the Episode: Episode 6 "His Visit: Day Five."
John from Cincinnati website. December 2007.

Some techniques, like the obscuring of faces, can make an image
more interesting.

Pay attention to the
breath when naming
a product.

The mystical power of names runs from the Jewish prohibition on saying the divine's name to Ursula K. Le Guin's short speculative story "The Rule of Names."

And Western thought has many theories on the origin of names. In Plato's *Cratylus* a dialogue argues whether names have a natural connection to the object named, or are they a product of convention? Ultimately the text is at a loss to the answer. Knowledge through words is both possible and impossible. Names conceal and reveal at the same time. And, somehow, their imprecision is truthful and reveals being.

Naming in contemporary branding leans toward the conventional. Even if they are onomatopoeic, names need to be agreed upon—often by committee—so, by default, they are conventional. This most likely describes why the names of pharmaceutical brands are so kludged together.

Rather than parsing along the lines of the *Cratylus*—natural versus conventional names—or believing in the magical incantational power of words; perhaps there's another way to think about naming a brand: write with the breath.

Over the last century, American poets Allen Ginsberg and Charles Olson both emphasized the importance of the breath. This seems archaic given that most writing today is done via the keyboard. But if we go back to the wandering lyric poets of Plato's time, as well as cultures in every corner of the world, we see that poetry was intended to be performed in public.

Writing with the breath adds kinetic energy, which is something a good namer will attend to: the force of the word, the vector of the syllables, the line of the overall form. In his "Projective Verse," which was first published as a pamphlet, Olson says that listening to the breath "is to engage speech where it is least careless—and least logical."[1] In other words, emotion, which is the domain of brand.

One of the more notable brand names in recent years is the Bluetooth speaker company Sonos, developed by Lexicon in Oakland, California. It has a conventional relevance (coming from the words "sound" and "sonic"), a natural quality (the mouth becomes an open audio chamber, like a speaker), and the word, when spoken, has a vector that ends in the sound of the wind. The wind: one of the first mystical powers to stir the mind and heart of humanity.[2]

Notes:
1. Charles Olson. "Collected Prose." 1997. University of California Press. Oakland, California.
2. See 54. Magic and Superstition, 46. How You Say It.

The name "Sonos" is relevant (reflecting the words "sound" and "sonic"), natural (the mouth becomes a resonant chamber), and when spoken, mimics the wind.

If brand associations are developed over time, then time becomes an important factor.

While there are competing theories whether humans are born into, or develop an animist relationship with, the objects around us, the notion that objects are imbued with some kind of a soul is both ancient and contemporary. In his famous *Remembrance of Things Past*, Marcel Proust describes a Celtic belief that the souls of the dead are held captive in an animal, plant, or object, lost until the day when we come upon that particular prison and hear them call out. Once we recognize their voice, the spell is broken. The soul overcomes death and then returns to share our life.

There is a resonance between animistic belief and our relationship with branded objects. They arrive in quality-controlled perfection without scuff marks, fingerprints, or any sign of prolonged human contact. Their presence, direct from the factory, is as imagined. But once that first scratch or blemish appears, once the pure white begins to yellow, once it gets dropped and dented, once it is used with a significant other the object merges with the owner's memory and takes on a more intimate role.

Our possessions anchor us in time and place and situate us in society. As Proust would use a frayed sleeve to tell the wearer's story, we interpret other people by the brands they choose to live with. And personally, as we clean out a closet or go through childhood toys, we reencounter earlier, different versions of ourselves.

The word nostalgia is a combination of the Greek words for "homecoming" and "ache." The feeling is usually triggered sensorially: a smell, a piece of music, an old book. Positive nostalgic feelings can consolidate memory, make people feel connected, and help deal with loss.

There are numerous examples of the strategic manipulation of nostalgia in advertising or product design. Vintage design motifs in Coca-Cola products, Budweiser replacing its name with the word "America," and Gap ads featuring historical figures in khakis are some of the better-known. And all are connected with tactile objects.

The digital order has deobjectified contemporary life and will definitely have an effect on memory and nostalgia. One can easily build a list of objects, procedures, and jobs that have been digitized and moved into the black rectangles we keep in our pockets. The challenge now is how to build rich brand associations in a virtual space without the aid of smell, taste, or touch; without gravity's pull; or without the effect of time on materials. And the question remains whether there will ever be a nostalgia for ordering food through an app, an hour spent scrolling through Instagram, or attending an event in the metaverse.

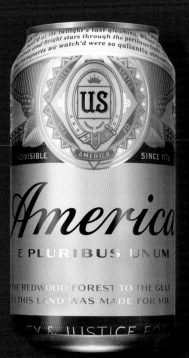

In the summer of 2016, Budweiser replaced its name on labels with the word "America." The remainder of the text used phrases from the Pledge of Allegiance and lyrics from "The Star Spangled Banner" and "America the Beautiful."

How culpable are brands in the devastation of our environment?

In the world of antiques, graphic design is filed under "printed ephemera." Even though ink-on-paper outlives digital files by dozens, if not hundreds, of years, print is still considered ephemeral—used for a short period of time, easily recycled, and just as easily forgotten. And in that context, there can be a certain thrill for a graphic designer to see their work in the trash. The piece has been fully digested by the system and excreted. It has done its job.

Unfortunately this ease of disposal is in itself ephemeral. The chemicals that allow printed material to appear on a bright white, smooth surface in a vivid and, at times, opaque color are all pollutants. Their presence, while invisible to the end user, remains in the environment.

This focus on a brief intersection—the first impression, the sale, the packaging— has had an equally harmful effect for over a century. And this effect expands into the manufacture of pretty much everything beyond printed ephemera. Along with almost magical developments in the material sciences, humanity's mindset has transformed the natural world into a standing reserve of resources ready to be ordered, broken down, and reconfigured into perfect expressions of our creativity. Everything, everywhere—including human beings themselves—is now a resource to exploit.

Sustainability is an increasing concern for producers and consumers alike. Phrases like "cradle to cradle" describe a mindset where garbage becomes a resource in a production chain. A chain that attempts to consider future generations but still begins with a natural resource.

It is so naturally easy to throw things away without a second thought. We have been trained to do so with such efficiency and rewarded with more wonderful things to take their place. But as long as sustainability is used as a differentiator between products—as a point to advertise, ultimately—and as we continue to give ourselves permission to consume, humanity will continue to destroy the world.

There is a profound opportunity for the branding profession to help dismantle rampant consumerism. The profession is often coupled with capitalist production and consumption, but this is only part of its potential. Who says that the purpose of branding is only to get people to buy stuff they don't need? Can't there be a higher purpose? If branding aligns people into a unified mindset, what would happen if it also extolled the virtues of producing, consuming, and having enough? Because the continued flourishing of life on Earth is probably the most urgent brand right now.

Products purchased online may magically appear at the door,
but their production and delivery have environmental effects.

The ability to track the interstitial flows of attention and behavior promises to offer more-nuanced customer data.

When strategists analyze consumer or market behavior, they engage across two broad research categories: quantitative or qualitative.

Quantitative, or "quant," examines data points pulled from a large sample size. The questions that are asked tend to be highly structured and specific because the goal is to collect numerical data, which will then be subject to statistical analysis. The United States Census is a good example of a quant study that analyzes the American population in order to track, along with basic numbers of people, their movement across the country, the increasing complexity of racial identity, and trends in household makeup. That data helps allocate government spending and determine legislative representation.

In theory, a quant survey is more objective than a qualitative ("qual") one. But as the increasing arguments about which questions are asked in the U.S. Census show, the intentions of the programmer are revealed in the program. Even such a seemingly harmless survey, like tracking the percentage of attendees who pay for concessions at a sporting event with a smartwatch, has layers of assumptions about socioeconomic status embedded within.

Qualitative surveys openly place researchers directly into the area of study. They investigate more deeply into individual motivations with open-ended questions (never a "yes" or "no") and the ability to ask follow-up questions that are specific to the respondent.

It's easy to think of quant and qual as binaries at extreme points along a scale. One is numbers, while the other is narrative. One objective, the other subjective. But the two are intertwined. A good example is water. As the quant of water temperature changes, the qual of its state changes: ice becomes water becomes steam. The two types of data are both incomplete descriptions of an object as it becomes something else.

One may claim that a general theory of society must be a generalized theory of flows. This idea is embedded in the work of economist John Maynard Keynes, who spoke of the circular flow of money. One person's spending goes towards another's earnings, and when that person spends her earnings she is, in effect, supporting another's earnings.

But we also live in an economy of attention and behaviors.

Basing insights on samples, like demographic segmentations or customer interviews, may be tempting, but that doesn't convey the complete picture. Consumer insights are not just about the consumer at a moment in time. They are about both the consumer and the business acting within a larger ecosystem, i.e., the world at large.

There is even more of a need for consumer observation to consider states of change measuring vectors rather than samples. This kind of work requires a nonsiloed holistic approach to a world of fragmented audiences, chaotic environments, and disconnected data.

Can liminal states, like distraction, fit into the analysis of market or customer behaviors?

This is the worst approach to rebranding.

As brands develop, as time progresses, and as different personalities cycle through various positions, it's natural for an organization's structure to become complex and fragmented. Such a situation becomes an ideal breeding ground for redundancies, inefficiencies, and internal conflicts.

Brands have a choice at this moment. Either they can undergo a protracted brand architecture project—a complicated assessment, reorganization, and repositioning that might take more than a year and may alienate internal stakeholders—or they can take the simpler route. They could announce an initiative with the name "One (name of the company)."

These sorts of initiatives are easily found with a simple online search. Type in the word "one" followed by the name of a company or organization with a wide multiregional presence and chances are that they have made such an attempt.

"One _____" is very common in financial services but generally as an internal effort. There was One Citi in 2007, One HSBC ("a common technology platform across business units and regions") in 2008, One Credit Suisse ("aimed at showing how the company can serve the needs of different clients") in 2009, One Wells Fargo in 2010, One Chase ("a journey to create an outstanding customer experience in everything we do") in 2011, and One Goldman Sachs in 2020.

The phenomenon appears in professional organizations: One AIGA (American Institute of Graphic Arts) in 2013, and One AMA (American Medical Association) in 2019. And multinational corporations have tried consumer-facing campaigns as well: One GE (General Electric) in 2005, One Google in 2016, and We Are One Starbucks in 2022.

It may be common, but the One _____ direction rarely results in effective change. There is no well-defined call to action, ideal state, or unifying theme. Just saying that an organization is One _____ doesn't make it so. The power of the C-suite goes only so far.

The one effective result of a One _____ initiative is to point out an organization that probably should consider taking a closer look at their brand. If there is a lack of unity, then there probably isn't a strong association connecting employees or customers to the brand. To anyone with a degree of experience in branding, One _____ is most likely a temporary fix. Because strong, effective associations are rarely made by edict.

Note:
See 11. Brand Architecture.

Top: Logo designed by Milton Glaser for a 1977 campaign to promote tourism in New York State.
Bottom: 2023 version of the 1977 campaign, created for the Partnership for New York City.

When advertising conveys brand messaging; situational advertising may be a better approach.

Advertising is a hungry beast. It is constantly on the lookout for the audience's attention and new territories. As traditional magazine readership and broadcast viewership declined and technological innovations upended basically everything, the advertising industry has been forced to change in every way. Advertisers need to be much more agile in their approach, capable of pivoting and responding at the speed of social media. Additionally algorithmically powered digital delivery has changed the focus from selling a (new and improved) product to the customer (personalization).

This means that the message of advertising has evolved into brand awareness and problem solving. The line between brand and advertising has become blurred, which offers an opportunity to examine that in-between area.

One advertising sector in that space is out-of-home (OOH), which is exactly what it sounds like: advertising experienced outside the home. It ranges from billboards and posters to bus stops, spots found within public transit to actual store fronts and an amorphous category known as either alternative or guerilla.

Some of the more clever guerilla OOH ads come from companies like BarkBox, a subscription service that delivers a customizable box of dog toys and treats every month. It cleverly affixed small stickers on lampposts, hydrants, or any other pieces of street furniture at the height of a dog's genitals. As a dog relieved itself, or smelled what another dog left, hopefully the owner would see that the message was perfectly targeted and eventually connect that precision with the brand's offerings.

But things become interesting when a brand's normal behavior is programmed to be basically an ad for itself. For example, in the 2021 Christmas software update, Tesla introduced the "Light Show" in its electric cars. This function illuminates all the lights on the car, and can open the trunk and windows, all choreographed to the music playing on the sound system. And its open-sourced platform allows users to program and share their own Light Shows.

Tesla famously does not advertise in the traditional sense; seeing their showrooms is all the marketing required. And there is a halo effect from company chairman Elon Musk's other activities in SpaceX, solar energy, battery development, and social media. But the company benefits from the still-strange sight of a Light Show in person or social media posts of users' cars performing customized Light Shows, sometimes with small groups of young men (always men) dancing around the car like members of a Tesla tribe.

According to Amazon founder Jeff Bezos, "Your brand is what other people say about you when you're not in the room." And in the case of Tesla, this new ability to program a car to perform places it in that area between brand and advertising: drawing attention and establishing specific associations about the company and its customers.

Tesla superchargers act as OOH advertisements for the vehicles.

People making fun of your
brand may be a
good thing.

To a graphic designer, there are fewer greater pleasures than seeing one's work in another person's collection: on their bookshelf, in their pantry, or in their record collection. For brands, perhaps that point is where the brand, and its messaging, has been so fully assimilated that it becomes the source of parody.

In November 2013 a commercial for Volvo trucks featuring the action-movie star Jean-Claude Van Damme was released. In it, Van Damme is performing one of his trademark splits, suspended between two Volvo trucks, while in voiceover he speaks about engineering, the laws of physics, physical perfection, and the mindset of mastery. It was an audacious, memorable spot—and a perfect target for parody.

Soon after, the Hungarian animation firm Delov Digital distributed a holiday greeting with fellow action-movie star Chuck Norris doing a split between two flying airplanes but with several men balanced on top of his head in the shape of a Christmas tree.

In advertising such references and remixes are known as earned media. It used to be the relatively exclusive domain of publicity and news reports, but in the digital realm, earned media now includes Yelp reviews, TikTok reels, and any other appearance in social media.

Previously if an individual uploaded their take on a piece of brand communication, the company's lawyers would send a cease-and-desist letter. But now the potential for collaboration is more likely. This is because more people trust what they learn from friends and family. Earned media ends up being more trustworthy.

Of course, this applies only to messages that are received positively. Pepsi's commercial of April 2017 featuring model Kendall Jenner was pulled after just one day. In it, Jenner steps away from a photo shoot to join, and eventually lead, a nonspecific protest that happens to be passing by. As the ethnically diverse crowd is met by a line of police, Jenner picks up a can of Pepsi and hands it to one of the officers, who drinks it. Everyone celebrates.

The ad, viewed as a cynical appropriation of the Black Lives Matter movement, was widely reviled. And one month later, during May Day demonstrations across the country, marchers were seen offering Pepsi to police officers. The brand's attempt to resurrect the "Pepsi Generation" of the 1960s had ended up erasing that association from people's minds.

Jean-Claude Van Damme performing one of his trademark splits
during a 2017 press conference in Munich, Germany.

Direct brand messaging, delivered personally, may be the best approach.

The image of a salesman soliciting business by going door-to-door is archetypal and the subject of countless jokes, cartoons, films, and television programs. But over time social mores, algorithms, and now COVID, have transformed the profession to the point where it exists more in a business-to-business (B2B) context than a direct-to-consumer one. And salespeople operating at a B2B level tend to have a smaller target market, which allows them to know their customer better and build deeper relationships.

A personal connection with the customer is one of the foundations of modern advertising. In the 1930s, before opening a firm that went on to dominate the advertising industry, David Ogilvy was a door-to-door salesman for the AGA cooking stoves. His learnings from that experience—continual research, knowing the product, building rapport and trust, and persistence—were published as *The Theory and Practice of Selling the Aga Cooker.* While its language may not have aged well, it was identified in a 1971 issue of *Fortune* magazine as "probably the best sales manual ever written."

Today anyone working in advertising or marketing who began selling door-to-door is more the exception than the rule. While not a requirement for success, such an experience does teach one how to interact with real people instead of with abstract data points.

Instead of armies of door-to-door salesman going out to meet potential customers, we now have experiential marketing. It could be as viral as an "influencer" ordering a new liquor at a bar, then speaking to the people next to them about the product or buying them a drink. Or it could be some sort of event where the customer comes to them, either at a temporary pop-up shop or a hospitality tent at a larger event.

Regardless of the scale, such experiential marketing really only meets the "awareness" stage of the customer journey. If anything, people will more likely remember the party and not the brand. And given the temporary nature of much experiential marketing, it runs the risk of portraying a product in a bad light. The space may have been so quickly put together that it looks more like an amateur theater set than a considered and polished experience.

Experiential marketing, done properly, requires an investment in time and money. More successful efforts, like Samsung's 837NYC, is more than a store. It is an interactive playground featuring products, art installations, and Samsung-related experiences. Such an experience connects back with David Ogilvy's principles of knowing the product and building rapport and trust with the customer.

Note:
See 86. Talk to the Gatekeepers.

An early example of experiential marketing is the Wienermobile, used to promote and advertise Oscar Mayer products in the United States. The first vehicle was created by Oscar Mayer's nephew, Carl G. Mayer, in 1936.

The best brands allow people to say "yes."

Brands aren't always about consumption or selling. They are mental associations and connections. To that end, perhaps one should think about a brand's personality.

Each brand, like each person, has a distinctive personality. But rather than immediately diving into specificities and differences, sometimes it helps to step back and think in a wider manner.

A good approach is to look for the more open-ended aspects of the brand. Instead of "What does it do?, What is it made of?, What does it look like?," or even, "Is it politically-aligned?" ask what it allows. This question speaks to possibility and invites a variety of responses.

There seems to be longevity in permission. Permission maintains open territory for future growth, where regulations and restrictions do not. Permission makes room for what otherwise would be considered off brand.

Nike gives permission to its audience to be active, regardless of their athleticism, body type, or ability. Which is why we see people of all shapes and sizes wearing Nike. As opposed to Dolce & Gabbana, which only slightly increased their size offerings in 2019—a move that gained much attention. Prior to that, one's body had to conform to Dolce & Gabbana standards in order to participate in the brand.

A sense of permission shifts the brand's values away from an insistence on a standard model into an acceptance of the reality of the world, as lived by real people. Granted the permissions afforded by consumer-packaged goods may not be as open as a lifestyle brand, but with an open mind, who knows?

For example, Kraft Macaroni & Cheese has offered brand extensions into mac and cheese–flavored gummy candy, ice cream, and candy. These may not appeal to everyone's taste, but that sense of permission can also extend into how the base product is prepared, whether it be on a barbeque, with the addition of lobster, or turned into a dessert.

Permission allows one to say, "Yes." Obviously we don't want to say "yes" to everything, but keeping an open door, and an open mind, to opportunities for a brand to flourish is certainly a growth mindset. It is also a good gambit in the early stages of the customer journey. How can we give our audience permission to use the brand, or to imagine themselves as part of the brand? Such a mindset is less about consumption and more about the gift of possibilities.

Note:
See 23. Customer Journey.

Clockwise from top left: Kraft Mac & Cheese main product packaging, cobrand with Van Leeuwen ice cream, and Kraft Mac & Cheese prepared with a candy flavor packet to turn the mac & cheese pink and add hints of sweet candy flavor.

There is an argument for maintaining a sense of play when developing a brand.

If one wanted to distill the practice of branding into a single descriptive word, perhaps that word would be "framing." Branding concerns itself with how things are distinguished or "framed." And the more distinctive the framing, the more effective the brand.

The creative act of positioning a brand is basically a mental act, a bit of thinking that benefits from what the Maltese psychologist Edward de Bono called "lateral thinking." Such thinking avoids classic $A + B = C$–style logic in favor of intuition, humor, and play. The goal of such thinking is to disrupt routine approaches and to allow for a wider variety of inputs and associations, which could redirect the process in a new direction.

While it may be difficult to establish a scientifically validated claim for the benefits of lateral thinking, there are theoretical precedents that underscore its importance. The British pediatrician and psychoanalyst Donald Winnicott, building upon the work of Sigmund Freud and Melanie Klein, described the importance of play in child development. To him, the "desultory formless functioning" of the "unintegrated state" (aka play) was a source of creativity. In other words, allowing oneself to just drift, free of requirements and obligations, establishes the ideal creative situation.

In time-managed corporate structures, unintegrated play is dangerous. It resists being accounted into billable hours, thus framing it as unprofessional behavior. What client would willingly pay for "play time?" Instead teams attempt to manage the chaos of unintegrated thinking into a regulated game known as brainstorming.

Brainstorming is the opposite of play. Pulling groups of people together for a structured ideation session establishes a tacit political order to the process and its output. Participants will most likely moderate their contributions based upon their own perception of agency and power, and the process will reflect those preexisting relationships. The word itself—"ideation"—carries the expectation of a tangible product at the other end of the process.

Ideation locks things down. It frames thinking into a digestible, client-facing process that produces actionable results. It requires an outcome, where play does not. The open-ended cloud of play may not have a direct linkage to an execution or tactic, but it does establish a mindset and a practice. Its unintegrated cousins include meditation, cleaning, walking, showering, or any other liminal state suspended between beginning and ending. The goal is to allow ideas to come and go on their own accord and to frame a space where that may happen.

Brainstorming is the opposite of play. There is a political order to the process, which reinforces routine approaches and results.

All brands need to keep an eye on the political ramifications of their actions.

There are three categories of human activity. Labor is concerned with the continuity of life: acquiring food and shelter, cooking, raising children, etc. Work is the maintenance of relationships mediated through objects: building, supplying, regulating, teaching, etc. And action is the collective plurality of labor and work: politics, history, culture, etc.

Each level of activity conditions us to a life amongst a wide variety of other sensibilities, with labor and work laddering up from the locally political to a wider impact. Even the smallest activity reflects a political reality.

Regardless of their intention, brands also express a political position. And in today's current social media environment, that position has never been more transparent or documented. Supply chains and resources are examined for any trace of exploitation or conflict of interest, as are manufacturing methods, financial connections, and labor policies. If any perceived offense is found, it is immediately brought to the court of public opinion.

This creates a condition for brands that is both perilous and reveals opportunities. Political winds shift with increasing frequency. That which was acceptable a year ago may now be seen as offensive. Preexisting contractual arrangements, celebrity endorsement contracts, or even naming conventions made in one political climate continually run the risk of becoming liabilities. Constant vigilance is required, lest someone outside the brand discover it first.

Simultaneously political turmoil provides numerous opportunities for brands to signal their ethical positions. The risk is in aligning oneself with a figure or cause, which can backfire. Jared Fogle, who lost 245 pounds (111 kg) while eating food from Subway, spent fifteen years as the company's spokesperson—until he was arrested for the possession of child pornography.

There are "comfort food" positions as well. A brand aligns with a cause that doesn't require too much thinking or doesn't create too much controversy. These actions may satisfy the board's desire to take a stand without really taking a stand, but their ease has little longevity. It's a quick hit of satisfaction but doesn't do much to gather people into the brand's "tribe."

If all action reflects a political reality, then brands need to think deeply about how they exist in the world. Labor, work, and action all contribute to the continuity of life. Labor continues the species, and work establishes a durability of our activity over time. But action, the political, is where our endeavors begin to find permanence.

Aligning an audience into some sort of political sphere can resonate longer than many touchpoints. For example, the Pepsi Generation continues to exist in some form. We may not know what it means exactly, but we know how it makes us feel. And "good things come to those who wait," which began as a Guinness slogan, echoes in the lessons bestowed upon children today.

Starbucks advertisement originally developed in 2002 by Thomas Prowell. The tribute runs annually with slight revisions to the text. This version says "It's time to look at things differently. Again."

PROFESSIONALISM SECOND

A gentle reminder to brand professionals to practice professional humility.

Upholding the customs and conventions of expected workplace behavior is both good etiquette and the basic definition of professionalism. At the same time, professionalism is responsible for the general improvement of all methods and processes and the very thing that hinders that progress. Because it is a standard against which we evaluate ourselves and others, corresponding to compensation and reward, we need to be wary of its pitfalls.

The domain expertise that accompanies professionalism frequently leads to "siloization." It is easier, and safer, to stay in one's appointed position. We know how to act toward coworkers based upon their job title. A person from accounting receives an appropriate accounting-like response, and a "creative" receives an appropriate creative-like response in turn. We then expect people to respect the boundaries around our own titles.

"How dare they suggest a typeface? Don't they know I'm the design expert on this project?"

If branding's power lies in authentic feelings of connection, then the branding professional's relationship to ego needs to be in balance. Developing a brand requires planning. And the intellectual act of planning funnels through an expertise regulated by both professional standards and the ego.

The value of one's work is tracked through notoriety, profit, and attention, which all contribute to a sense of professionalism. This external feedback may be easier to measure and appreciate, but it can limit as well. The number of Cannes Lions or Design & Art Direction (D&AD) pencils on one's mantle tells only a small part of an ephemeral story. There will always be another round of winners next year. And award categories, and their winners, are always subject to obsolescence.

Perhaps the best measure of a brand's effectiveness is its effect on language. As incandescent lightbulbs are phased out in favor of more efficient, brighter technologies like the LED, the bulb itself will likely remain as a metaphor for an idea. Zippers, dumpsters, ping-pong, and Velcro are all words that have transcended their brand name origins to become ways in which we describe the world. Brands are not one thing; they are everything, uniting across the domains of history, economics, politics, culture, and language. Their existence is interdisciplinary, and their development should be as well. Professionalism is well-suited for tactical execution—a design, a strategy, an analysis—but remember that there is always a larger goal.

If someone outside your domain makes a suggestion or asks an "uninformed" question, try not to see it as an attack but rather as a gift. It is an opportunity to clarify, reach outside your silo, and make that connection.

"Siloization" prevents true collaboration and reinforces the norms
within each professional domain.

Brands mediate human relationships.

If ever there was a case to be made for the importance of design, it's the role of designed objects as mediators of human relationships. We sit in (designed) chairs, around (designed) tables, over (designed) meals, and engage in relationships with others.

The first human to pick up a stick or stone as a means to an end set in motion a sequence that developed into design practice. And those designed objects are now conceived, distributed, and consumed in constructs known as brands. Branded objects and, at a larger scale, brands themselves mediate human interaction.

Besides their basic tool-use function, there is an exhibition value to brands that establish power relationships. The way in which a person is dressed, whether they have the most up-to-date smartphone, what kind of car they drive are all contributing factors in how another person interacts with them.

Keeping this in mind opens an opportunity for brands and branding professionals to view their audience as more than a means to an end (aka, a source for profits and returns). What would happen if the creation, distribution, and consumption of a brand was seen as an opportunity to truly acknowledge the end user? To see each interaction as an opportunity for a gift? To see each decision or judgment call as an opportunity to improve their well-being, no matter how small? If politics is the art of the possible, then this is the political potential of brands.

It's quite a responsibility, isn't it?

Then why is it that our system of production is so geared toward the bottom line? Short-term returns come at the expense of long-term relationships, which is counter to the relationship-building ethos of branding. If brands, and the objects associated with those brands, are the mediators of our interpersonal interactions, then perhaps there is a higher-order responsibility in how the audience is met, the small graces offered, the delights discovered in use. Brands, like writing, extend beyond our lives and live on beyond the lifespan of their creators. Whether the company continues to exist or not, the intention remains.

French architect Jean Nouvel's intention for the Louvre Museum in Abu Dhabi was to create "a welcoming world serenely combining light and shadow, reflection and calm." It also "aims to emphasize a fascination generated by the rare encounter" of Middle Eastern and European aesthetics.

A brand's environmental obligation includes how it appears in public space.

In 2006 the city of São Paulo, Brazil, passed the *Lei Cidade Limpa* (clean city law), which prohibited outdoor advertising and large signage in front of businesses. The resulting effect is quite striking—and slightly disorienting. We are so used to seeing advertising in the public sphere that it exists in an almost liminal state: not quite conscious nor unconscious. Where before we would use trees, hills, and buildings when giving directions, we now turn left at the Starbucks or go one street past McDonald's without giving a second thought to the brand.

This sort of tension between outdoor advertising and governmental control is not a new event. There are times when an exuberance of advertising—New York's Times Square, Piccadilly Circus, Las Vegas, or Shibuya Crossing—creates a certain aesthetic thrill. Such locations help establish who we are as a community, give texture to our common existence, and create a collective manner of expression. And there are situations when a cacophony of brand messages becomes an eyesore, with numerous logos scattered across the façade of a generically designed shopping center, location and sizes determined by financial arrangement. It is the latter which provokes local and state governments to regulate advertising, with examples like the U.S. Highway Beautification Act of 1965 and more recent legislation in Barcelona and Hawaii.

Perhaps we can look at the advertising/visual pollution tension as a modern version of Catholic Baroque versus Protestant Reformation architecture. To compete with the simplicity and approachability of Protestant churches (and the services within), the Baroque response was to overwhelm through the shock and awe of scale, detail, ornamentation, and gilded surfaces. Congregations were drawn to, and inspired by, the theatricality of the space.

The need to legislate advertising and signage obviously stems from landscapes ruined by rapacious consumerism. Humanity hasn't presented itself favorably in all the shopping plazas filling up the empty spaces between towns or the billboards that loom disproportionately over smaller structures. But advertising, signage, and logos are also part of our collective heritage. These artifacts, which are born in the frictionless perfection of the mind, require a particular kind of nurturing as they enter the real. One which holistically considers social and environmental contexts.

At one moment in the Bible a question is asked if a follower should pay taxes to Caesar. The response—give to Caesar what is Caesar's, and give to God what is God's—doesn't portray a binary opposition. It is a both/and situation. Balancing the needs of the brand with the social needs of public spaces can solidify the bonds found within the brand's audience and the community.

Current state of the Queens Place Mall, in Elmhurst, Queens, New York City. Designed in 1965 by Skidmore, Owings & Merrill, one of the most significant architectural firms in the world, it now has an unfortunate collection of misproportioned logos on the façade.

The wear and tear of a product, plus the ability to repair it, are a significant aspect of a brand.

Because they are often associated with production and marketing, brands are also tied to the idea of the new and improved. The hit of dopamine on purchase or the tingle of excitement upon first use are physio-psychological thresholds limited to the beginning of one's relationship with a product or service. The imagined potential is still in the mind, unsullied by the actual experience, and free of decay or entropy, which helps explain the term "retail therapy." Getting new things just feels good.

In such a mindset, novelty drives consumption; but COVID-related supply chain issues and environmental concerns revealed this to be unsustainable. And eventually that way of thinking leads to a waning of affect, where the joy of consumption begins to have less of an impact.

As products become more complex, producers have argued that their coding and development now fall under intellectual property law. If a car needs repair, the owner is required to bring it to a dealer because only they have access to diagnostic and service software. That may be understandable, but then how does replacing a cracked screen by anyone other than the dealer violate a smartphone's warranty? Going through the dealer can be just as expensive as buying a new one—which is probably part of the plan.

For over a decade, there has been growing social and legislative pressure for the consumer's right to repair electronic devices—either by themselves or with a third party. And COVID lockdowns helped fuel this reassessment. People had time to bake their own bread, darn clothing, or engage in any number of crafts.

Rather than chasing the new, perhaps there is something positive about adjusting our relationships with the objects we already have. Rather than replacing something that is broken or worn, how would repairing it affect that relationship? The ability to repair a possession is a boost to self-confidence, transforms the relationship of owner to object—and thus, transitively, transforms the relationship of the consumer to the brand.

Beyond boosting the consumer's self-image, the design, production, and distribution of reparable products or even products that improve with age (leather goods being a great example) can have a beneficial effect for a brand in a number of ways. It reduces supply chain pressure, is a positive step towards sustainability, and can alleviate the perception that the company is trying to squeeze every little bit of profit from the consumer.

Blue jeans communicate externally to other people, as well as back to the wearer. And that message is colored by the wear and tear of continual use.

Repetition of the same
brand messaging quickly
goes unnoticed.

We wear clothing every day, but we generally don't feel it because its familiarity to our skin doesn't demand our attention. But when its touch becomes strange or different enough—if it's ill-fitting, itchy, wet, or on fire—we notice.

Similar responses occur across all our senses. Anyone who lives near a highway offramp eventually no longer hears the traffic; residents of Richmond, Virginia, probably don't notice the sweet smell of tobacco in the air; and most people do not notice how doors to public spaces open out, while doors to private spaces open in. These things cease to be different enough to warrant our attention.

While we need to be familiar with something in order to be comfortable with it, being too familiar can either work for, or against, a brand. For example, Disney parks use two proprietary colors—Go-away Green and Blending Blue—to help disguise nonthematic structural elements like ductwork, fencing, and towers. Both are close enough to the colors of the landscape and the sky to avoid being noticed. Necessary structures are present but do not diminish the guest experience by being noticed.

When a customer-facing element is applied without this sensitivity, the effect tends to fall within two categories. It can be generic, like how motion picture trailers tend to blend into each other. Or it could be alienating, like how customer support representatives are required to follow a script. When a clerk finishes a transaction by robotically saying, "May I help the next guest?" it doesn't quite make one truly feel like a guest.

Thousands of details go into the concept and development of a brand. And the frequent focus is on how brand positioning is expressed visually, verbally, and materially. But not everything can be programmed or preplanned. And when things go wrong, they quickly spread across social media. The challenge then is to deliver an experience, which is familiar to the brand, in a way that allows each customer to feel seen as an individual. It could be as simple as allowing a variety of interactions, moments, sequences, or styles.

The musical term for this could be syncopation, which is a displacement of a regular beat that creates a sense of anticipation or forward movement. Robotically delivering the same brand experience can become dull quite quickly. Even consistent brands like Coca-Cola change their packaging or introduce a new line every once in a while. The challenge is in educating brand managers and representatives how to find the right balance between consistency and syncopation.

Disney's proprietary colors disguise nonthematic structural elements.
Top: Go-away Green on the structure's roof.
Bottom: Blending Blue on the retaining wall.

Brands emerge in the mind, not the eye.

Out of all the figures who have had a major impact on twentieth century art, Marcel Duchamp was among the most contrarian. Born into a well-educated and cultured family, Duchamp had two brothers who were also successful artists. Beginning in 1911, his brothers organized a regular discussion group of artists and critics, some of whom went on to make significant contributions to art and art theory.

As his work began to draw attention, and controversy, Duchamp began to question the role of ego and taste in his art. He stopped painting, took a job as a librarian, and began to study math and physics. Around the time of the first World War, Duchamp began to produce what he called "readymades"—everyday objects selected to become art. These included a bottle-drying rack, a snow shovel, and a urinal.

The readymades, and other conceptual pieces, were his attempts to make what he called "non-retinal" art—a concept he defined while speaking about Andy Warhol's paintings of Campbell's Soup cans as, "If you take a Campbell's Soup can and repeat it fifty times, you are not interested in the retinal image. What interests you is the concept that wants to put fifty Campbell soup cans on a canvas."

Duchamp's creative strategies, used to avoid conforming to his own taste, offer a valuable lesson for visual designers working in branding. If one takes an overview of design trends at any point in time, the similarity between pieces, and brands, is remarkable.

Similar typefaces, graphic effects, and layouts appear regardless of the brand or subject matter. Currently digital media has given designers the ability to create branding systems where typography stretches, snaps back, spins around in a circle, or suddenly all falls to the bottom of the screen. Each time the work is celebrated as groundbreaking, innovative, and experimental.

This "corporate experimentalism" flourishes because the majority of designers relegate themselves to the retinal. They serve the eye, which in turn satisfies the ego. They are the leaders of the profession, the young guns, feeding the rage for the new.

The innovations of corporate experimentalism are celebrated in industry award shows, which build the reputations of the studios and agencies where the work is produced and ultimately attracts clients. And in turn, awards shows slightly adjust their categories to match industry trends.

But every fashionable trend eventually goes out of style. There is always a new look soon to arrive. So instead of spending a Sisyphean eternity chasing new trends, why not step away and develop non-retinal branding systems? The results will definitely be surprising and may create even deeper brand associations.

In 1915 Marcel Duchamp selected a snow shovel as a readymade, titling it "In Advance of the Broken Arm." This, on the other hand, is a snow shovel, photographed with retinal intent. *Photo: Myers Creative Imaging.*

The value of ritual in branding.

It's not uncommon for brands to be associated with some sort of a ritual. As the objects in our lives situate us in time and culture, the rituals that we engage in make time livable. They are symbolic acts that establish communities and tie us to shared values. With ritual, time becomes structured and accessible. We have benchmarks to measure progress and set goals.

Rituals can be sacred—weddings, baptisms, pilgrimages—or they can be secular—elections, graduations, harvest festivals. But in each instance, the ritual is a shared symbolic, perhaps even transcendent, event. Ritual is not about production or consumption. It is about being fully present and fully in the moment.

Supreme sneaker drops trigger long lines of customers eager for a limited edition pair. Harry Potter midnight book releases saw similar lines of children dressed as wizards, anxious to get home for an early morning reading session. These, plus numerous other examples, are all connected to consumption, which is tied to some sort of production and marketing schedule. They are more routine instead of ritual.

Routine may give structure to time and existence—like a morning Starbucks, a lunchtime Sweetgreens bowl, or a SoulCycle session—but it does not symbolically connect individuals and community. This is not to say that brands are automatically exempt from meaningful rituals. For example, since 1924 Macy's has hosted the Thanksgiving Day parade in New York City. The event attracts millions of spectators, both in person and broadcast, and marks the beginning of the Thanksgiving holiday. And even though the last float in every annual parade features Santa—also marking the beginning of the Christmas shopping season—Macy's allows enough cognitive space for the parade to function as more of a social ritual than a marketing exercise. The inflation of parade balloons the night before has become another ritual, free of marketing, which attracts its own audience as well.

Between this event, and their almost-five-decade sponsorship of the annual American Independence Day fireworks over New York's East River, Macy's civic contribution through ritual probably makes them more vital to New York City than just about any other business.

Distinctions between ritual and routine are worth keeping in mind when proposing brand behaviors. Calling something a ritual may be received well in a client presentation, but consciously considering the symbolic and communal potential of an event or experience could be a way for a brand to become more essential than transactional.

Traditions like the regalia of the Household Troops and the Changing
of the Guard ceremony at Buckingham Palace contribute to the brand
known as Great Britain.

There are simple guidelines for branding professionals when writing a scope of work.

Branding's interdisciplinary nature makes scopes of work a necessary evil. Individual vendors, like photographers, can simply submit an estimate listing all equipment, expenses, and usage parameters. A scope, on the other hand, is more like an enhanced estimate that rationalizes costs and defines every step of a more involved process. If done correctly, a scope can become a marketing tool, setting the agency apart from the competition.

While every client, agency, and project is different, it is helpful to have a few generalized strategies in one's arsenal.

1. Avoid just designing a logo. Logos are the result of a thoughtful process. Anything less reinforces misperceptions about branding.

2. When negotiating long-term partnerships, consider proposing a basic time-and-materials approach instead of scoping every project. Eventually there will be a tiny request that takes less time to complete than the time to write and approve an individual scope. Note that this approach requires rigorous recording of hours, email threads, and receipts. Always expect an audit.

3. Break the scope into discrete phases of discovery, strategic and creative development, production/delivery, writing guidelines, and any deployment or training that may be required. Defining stages establishes benchmarks and billing phases and may be a way to distinguish the agency. Just don't trademark them as a proprietary process. That usually sounds silly.

4. Any due-diligence research done before winning the project falls outside the scope. It is the cost of doing business. If the client supplies research material, reporting out findings would be considered strategic development.

5. The open secret in branding is that even the biggest firms deploy small teams on even their largest global clients. The biggest cost to an agency is talent, and it is in their best interest to manage human resources. If you are a smaller agency, consider using this fact to your advantage. Same size team and expertise but in a more intimate working context.

6. Charging a percentage of the total fee (6 to 8 percent) for basic expenses and local travel is worth asking for. Nobody likes adding up receipts.

7. A client may think a too-round number (150,000 or 1 million) wasn't properly calculated. Consider taking a lesson from retail, where $14.99 is better than $15.00, and make the estimate slightly lower or higher.

8. Contingencies and politics will happen. Sometimes you need to add a little "focus the mind" money to the fee. The ability to know when this is appropriate develops over time.

9. A thoughtful program adds value to both client and agency. If it's worth using, it's worth paying for.

10. Scopes are conversations between equals. Honor your time, energy, and people. Keep the client's needs, limitations, and background in mind. Serve the larger audience.

[1] DISCOVERY

[2] DESIGN

[3] DEPLOYMENT

Writing a scope of work with three basic phases of discovery, development, and deployment establishes evaluation benchmarks and billing thresholds.

Brands change our language, which in turn changes our perception.

The absorption of trademarked names into our common vocabulary is basic human behavior, and the eternal struggle of intellectual property lawyers. Parker Brothers may have trademarked "Ping-Pong," but the word is frequently used to define any back-and-forth exchange, whether it be table tennis, verbal sparring, or a drunk walking down a hall.

The term for this consumption of meaning, "semantic infiltration," was coined by Swiss-American sociologist and foreign policy expert Fred Iklé. The original use described how political organizations appropriated terms from the opposite side and used them as a pejorative. Classic examples include any time a totalitarian regime calls themselves "freedom fighters" or "reformers." And, more recently, the American right uses "woke" (having a desire for social justice) and "ANTIFA" (anti-fascist) to describe what they consider to be imposed values, counter to individual freedom.

Such infiltration is not limited to language. The effects of products upon our bodies extend to our behavior, future products, and so on. Through the Victorian era, women's undergarments were much more rigid: whalebone corsets, bustles, hourglass silhouettes. Afterwards, through the 1920s, undergarments became less restrictive and silhouettes more androgynous. The way fabrics hung off the body and the way people moved took on a different character. This coincided with technological advances in sound and film recordings, which moved across racial lines, affecting everyday speech and, ultimately, society.

Another example of a brand infiltrating, and being infiltrated by, society begins in 1979, when Sony introduced the Walkman portable audio cassette player. Almost immediately, people's relationship to music and technology changed. Prior to the Walkman, portable music came in the form of transistor radios. You could listen, but the programming was out of your control. The Walkman allowed users to select exactly what they listened to and align their playlists to specific activities. One could have specific music for workouts, commuting, or shopping. And one could communicate via mixtape.

The writer Geoffrey O'Brien described the mixtape as "perhaps the most widely practiced American art form, that serves as self-portrait, gesture of friendship, prescription for an ideal party, or simply as an environment consisting solely of what is most ardently loved."[1]

As portable audio technology advanced, it became easier to program personal mixes, which then further altered our relationship with music. That which began in ritual became a commodity and is now an environmental feed. By giving us greater control over our audio environment—to the point where people no longer pay the sort of attention to music that they used to—the Walkman, as a product, became so ubiquitous its descendants are virtually invisible. But the Walkman, as a brand, changed the way we perceive our world.

Note:
1. Geoffrey O'Brien, *Sonata for Jukebox: An Autobiography of My Ears*, 2005, Counterpoint/Perseus Books, New York, NY.

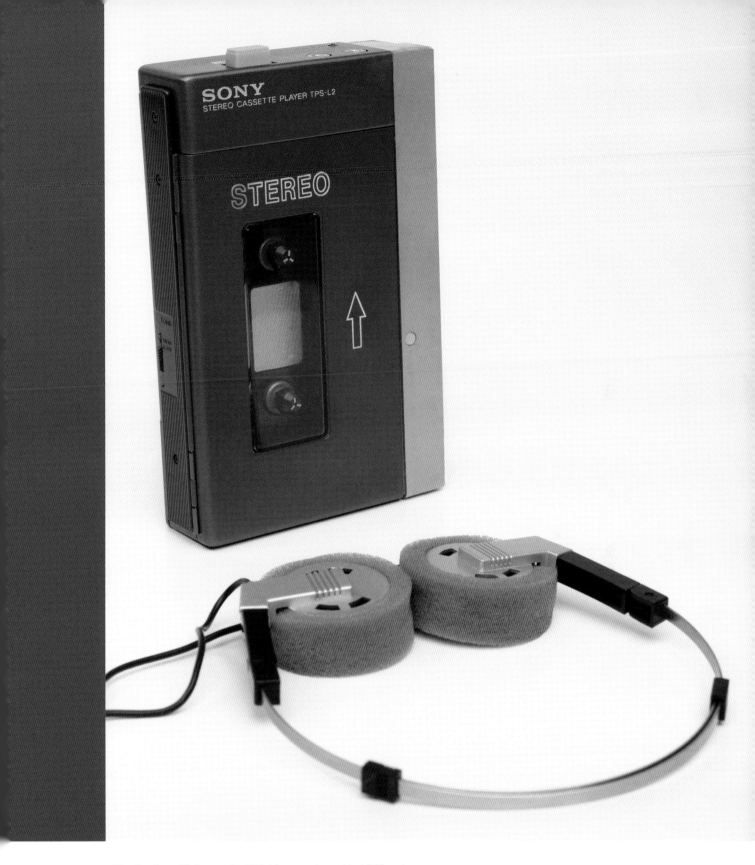

The first Sony Walkman, the TPS-L2, was released in 1979 and forever changed the way we perceive our world.

A brand is a higher-order semiotic process.

Throughout this book the comment that brands are associations in the minds of the audience is repeated frequently. Of course, they don't just magically appear this way. They need to be conveyed. And this is done through a process known as a sign. Defining and analyzing signs is an area of study known as semiotics.

There are numerous ways to describe the sign process, otherwise known as a semiosis. The American logician and pragmatist Charles Sanders Peirce saw a sign as a three-step process. It begins with the object (Peirce's naming convention), which is anything thinkable. The object is represented in a manner—a word, image, gesture, etc.—that can be interpreted. Finally that representation is decoded or interpreted.

If the interpretation aligns with the object, that is a closed semiosis. But if it does not align, then that can become a second representation, which sets up a new interpretation: ad infinitum. This is known as an open semiosis.

Next there are three general categories of signs. Iconic signs stand in for the object: a tree-shaped image or a smiley face. Indexical signs maintain a factual connection: a footprint or a skid mark. And symbolic signs utilize agreed-upon conventions: hearts for love or retirees walking hand-in-hand for financial planning.

There are no sharp distinctions between sign categories. A lipstick print on the bottom of a note is an iconic sign for a person's kiss, an indexical sign of their presence, and a symbolic sign of their affection.

So why does this matter to branding? Simply put, a sign does not exist unless it is acknowledged as a sign. Therefore, since brands signal all sorts of things—value, associations, personal identity, etc.—they are entanglements of signs, which collectively need to be seen as a brand in order to be a brand.

This realization shifts the process from monologue to dialogue. Brands are a constant dance of encoding/decoding between producer and consumer or between consumers and other consumers.

A circular ring of wear on a jean back pocket means the wearer chews tobacco and probably has a certain kind of employment, votes a certain way, and drinks beer rather than wine. We see the ring and make a host of assumptions about that person's place in branded culture. And chances are that person uses that tobacco ring to broadcast their own network of associations.[1]

Contemporary life is complex. And brands help us efficiently navigate that complexity. Yes, they have been put to use in order to increase sales, but they also facilitate the cognitive load required to be in the world.

Note:
1. Brand designer and strategist Chelsea Carlson engaged in a protracted analysis of chewing tobacco rings at the School of Visual Arts Masters in Branding program.

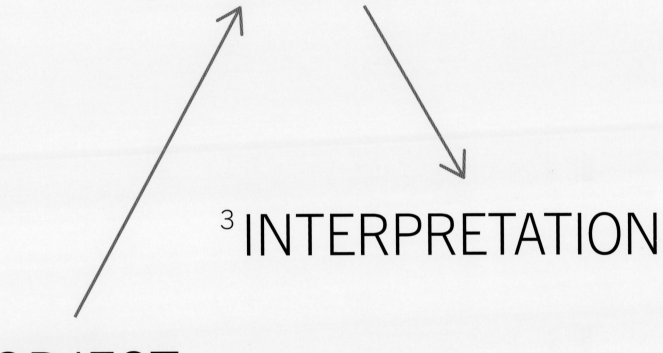

² REPRESENTATION

³ INTERPRETATION

¹ OBJECT

Charles Sanders Peirce's model of a sign as a three-step process,
also known as a "semiosis."

The branding profession is strengthened when practitioners focus their efforts on the greater good over short-term profit.

Currently branding has a branding problem. It is frequently seen as a profit-driven practice that motivates people to adapt inauthentic ideas, pursue false aspirations, and consume more. Part of this perception is driven by how people speak about branding, best exemplified in reality shows when someone (often engaged in an entrepreneurial effort) makes a comment about something being "good for their brand."

Examples like this reduce branding to an instrumental tactic at the expense of a role in the larger cultural conversation. Yes, the orchestrated coordination of visual, verbal, sonic, environmental, behavioral, etc. assets can enhance customer perception, engagement, and retention. But branding is also what humans do—whether we acknowledge it or not. Human activity is concerned with more than buying and selling—and so should branding.

So why do branding firms defer so easily to client whims? The average lifespan of a creative director within an agency tends to be eighteen to twenty-four months. And marketing people approximately last twice as long. This constant churn of players—all hoping to make their name somewhere, somehow—creates a situation where individual aspiration supersedes brand integrity. It's a familiar story: A new chief marketing officer joins a company, does a bit of analysis, and soon after begins a new initiative, which ends in a new logo, a new name, and a new positioning.

Compounding all this are the profit-and-loss requirements of the holding company model, which demands a set annual percentage increase. This incentivized firms into creating that new logo, name, and positioning, all in the name of annual growth.

Branding firms insist that a brand is a more stable phenomenon than a campaign, but in a sense, their willingness to take on these projects suggests that they don't believe what they preach.

A new visual identity system can easily convey a new energy in the brand. But that is a surface-level approach. Perhaps a more courageous and daring response that engages brand aspects that are operational, logistic, financial, or product based would result in an effective rebranding. If a brand is an association held in the audience's mind, then these behavioral changes might be more substantial than slapping "lipstick on a pig."

Such an approach elevates the branding profession to something more than the royal court equivalent of a cake decorator and makes it more of a true client partner. It certainly would help dispel the myth that branding is only a way to increase consumption.

1970–1986

1986–October 4, 2010

October 4–October 11, 2010

October 11, 2010–January 2010

January 2016–present

Evolution of the Gap logo. The 2010 iteration was so widely criticized,
the company reverted to the previous version after a week.

Brands can no longer avoid their social responsibility.

There used to be a thought that no two countries that had a McDonald's franchise would go to war with each other. The bonds of free-market enterprise were supposedly strong enough to give opposing parties enough of a commonality to overcome their differences.

In 2011, at the beginning of civil war in Syria, the French news and entertainment program *Le Petit Journal* aired a segment where a correspondent drove across the border from Lebanon into Syria. The host, Yann Barthès, and the correspondent commented on how just past a McDonald's billboard the road became pockmarked with craters caused by shelling. The McDonald's rule was obviously no longer in effect.

The past couple decades have seen more than their share of conflict; and because of their role in contemporary culture, brands are caught in the middle. Where once a brand could get away with the platitudes and bromides of supporting the common good, social fracturing, compounded by the immediacy of social media, mean that a brand can no longer hide.

Now, in a post–Arab Spring, post-Ukraine world where Extinction Rebellion, Occupy, and various freedom movements have increased social capital, brands can no longer pass with platitudes and bromides. It's more difficult for a brand to "be for" as wide an audience as possible. The pressure to be specific and clear in what they stand for, beyond their main offering, is intensified. And the ramifications for making such a declaration require new approaches that are beyond traditional marketing considerations.

In 2017, when the American football player Colin Kaepernick knelt during the national anthem as a protest of police brutality and racial inequality, he found himself blackballed, with no NFL team willing to sign him. Political pressure and the racial divide between team owners and players effectively ostracized him.

The following year, Kaepernick was featured in a Nike ad with the text, "Believe in something. Even if it means sacrificing everything." This seemed to conform with Nike's beliefs of personal agency and determination.

But when Nike celebrated the American Independence with an American flag motif, Kaepernick's public critique noted the flag's association (the American system itself) with slavery. Nike quickly pulled the product off the shelves, prompting further criticism from conservative political and media voices.

There is no easy approach to how a brand addresses its social responsibility. A positively received move one day can lead to a long-term decline later on. But the one certainty is that brands now need to look beyond just financial return and think deeply about their role in society.

An electronic billboard for Nike products featuring Colin Kaepernick, the American football player who knelt during the national anthem as a protest of police brutality and racial inequality.

What if your logo
was a drum pattern?

Two decades after the end of the Second World War, a generation of young German musicians developed a style of music known as Krautrock. Mixing avant-garde composition and recording techniques with the energy and attitude of popular music, it captured the hope of postwar Germany rebuilding itself in a new technological horizon. Krautrock bands like Can, Neu!, and Kraftwerk sound as fresh as when they first appeared, and their influence continues to this day.

A notable component of Krautrock was the 4/4 drumbeat known as "motorik," German for "motor skill." The motorik beat established a relentless, repetitive foundation upon which soaring melodies and long-held notes stretched out into an ideal future. A frictionless technological future full of possibility that expressed a uniquely cosmopolitan, modern sensibility.

If a logo and visual identity system can signal the feeling of a brand, then so can a drumbeat. And being more abstract and open to interpretation, it does a good amount of emotional work with great efficiency.

Current sonic branding practice is generally harmonic or melodic in approach. Think of Brian Eno's 1995 startup tone for Microsoft Windows (composed on a Macintosh, by the way) or Chase Bank ATM feedback cues. While lovely when heard once, one can imagine how annoying they might be when heard for the hundredth time.

The goal of sonic branding isn't necessarily to be included in the whistling repertoire of the common man but to contribute to a brand feeling. Mercedes-Benz vehicles are engineered to make a reassuring, solid "thud" when the door closes. While not a piece of music, the thud is still composed. And hearing that thud subconsciously connects the passenger to a tradition of quality engineering and manufacture and transitively to feelings of safety, speed, and reliability.

The possibilities for sonic cues are endless. Adjusting the width of corrugated cardboard, combined with a pull-tab seal, could give a distinctive tone, or sequence of tones, to a package when opened. The wheels on luggage could be engineered for total silence (wouldn't that be nice?) And a solid, heavy zipper with thicker teeth could make the wearer of a garment feel ready to meet the world.

Such sonic cues succeed or fail, depending on their context. Snapple Iced Tea bottles used to make a distinctive pop when opened. Supposedly a connection to freshness, the pop lost its context when Snapple switched from glass bottles to plastic. And now the product doesn't quite taste the same. It has lost that sense of promise found in motorik or in a Mercedes door and become a disconnected cue.

Klaus Dinger from the band Neu! on drums, 1970.
Superimposed: the basic Motorik beat.
Photo: Wolfgang v. Groote.

Brands have outgrown traditional visual identity standards.

Many confuse corporate identity with branding. Corporate identity is the standardization of a company's visual assets—logos, typefaces, color pallets, etc.—into a unified look and feel. It is generally considered to have begun around 1907, when architect Peter Behrens began his tenure as design consultant for the German company AEG (Allgemeine Elektricitäts-Gesellschaft). Over the following three decades, his studio output for the company included graphics, marketing campaigns, products, and factory buildings.

The year he began with AEG, Behrens joined a group of architects and industrialists in a state-sponsored effort known as the Deutscher Werkbund. Together they aspired to combine craft with industry in order to define a design and architectural market presence that was uniquely German.

Behrens' training was based on the traditional atelier model: the standard for European artistic and architectural production from the Middle Ages to the nineteenth century. It brought together assistants, students, and apprentices to work on projects supervised by, and released under the principal artisan's name. It is little wonder that Behrens' corporate identity work reflected both his interests in a unified and distinctive aesthetic taste, mixed with the central control of architectural practice.

This model continued into the graphic design studios of the mid-twentieth century, considered the golden age of corporate identity. Like the atelier, their output reflected a centralized control over how things were to look and feel. And the standards manuals produced during that time gave specific instructions on how a company's visual identity should be constructed, down to the smallest detail.

Now, with the advent of branding, the territory for standards manuals is widely expanding. Merging beyond the visual, and even beyond tone of voice and writing standards. It is not uncommon for a financial institution to issue standards on credit card design that also address the strategies behind those cards. Companies will define audio cues and mnemonics for kiosks and marketing communications. Environmental design standards—even though every space is different—will define materials and approaches, down to the choice of decorative plants. And customer interaction—the most fluid and unpredictable of touchpoints—may not be specifically definable, but there can be a company-wide approach.

The challenge for branding today is not to try to control every single detail of every single touchpoint—which is impossible—but to find a way to convey the brand beliefs with a consistent look, feel, tone, or "vibe." The model shifts from central command and control to empowering appropriate decisions.

In 2014, Order Design published a reissue of the 1970 *New York City Transit Authority Graphics Standards Manual*, originally designed by Massimo Vignelli and Bob Noorda of Unimark International.

Brand strategy operates
at four basic levels.

For such a simple word, strategy retains its mystery within branding. Few can confidently define strategy and its role.

Over the last sixty-plus years, there has been a great deal of thinking directed toward the formulation and practice of strategy on a business and organizational level. But the one definition of strategy that seems to have had the greatest effect comes from the American economist and professor Michael Porter, who wrote: "Competitive strategy is about being different. It means deliberately choosing a different set of activities to deliver a unique mix of value."[1]

This still feels incomplete. Being different is a value or a goal, but how does one go about being different? Perhaps one needs to better define strategic practice. In that case, strategy becomes a two-pronged activity. First one analyzes an existing context—market conditions, audience mindset, cultural trends, etc.—and then develops some sort of an insight. They then propose a new context—behaviors, values, market engagement, product line, offerings, etc.—intended to answer the stated needs or goals of the client. Within this framework, strategy becomes both an analytical and a generative practice.

Additionally—painting with a very wide brush—there are four degrees of strategy, depending on client needs and personal experience.

At the widest are management consultants who develop overall strategies for global businesses, governments, or institutions. The "big three" in this field are McKinsey & Company, Boston Consulting Group, and Bain & Company. Their work, while not technically branding, has a profound effect on how brands are built and delivered.

Next in level of detail are the "upfront" strategists. They filter insights gleaned from numerous data sets, interviews, and observations through personal frameworks and years of experience and propose varying ways of framing, positioning, repositioning, and explaining a brand. The general goal of an upfront strategist is to create a moment of punctuated equilibrium where perception changes.

Sometimes a strategist is called to be an apologist for creative work. This assignment often goes to more experienced strategists with deeper reputations, longer client relationships, and a degree of gravitas. As the work is shown, they rationalize why it is an appropriate response and offer any antecedents or case studies as proof. Basically, they help sell creative work.

And at the most detailed level is what is commonly referred to as "donkey work." This is where reams of data, interviews, client documents, focus group results are compiled into material that fuels the previous three levels. It may not be the most glamorous, but it is a vital contribution to a well-integrated team's output.

Note:
1. Porter, Michael E. 1996. "What is a strategy?" *Harvard Business Review* (November–December).

The American economist and professor, Michael Porter.

Good taglines enhance a
brand's strategy.

The idea that a logo is not a brand is, thankfully, now generally accepted. A logo is a representation, a mnemonic device that can trigger an appropriate brand association. And, verbally, a tagline has a similar function. For lack of a better term, a tagline is a verbal logo.

The differences between a tagline, a strapline, and a slogan are not always clearly defined. And people use them interchangeably. But for this discussion a tagline, also known as a strapline, is a short phrase that captures the essence of a brand's character. And a slogan is a summarizing phrase in a marketing campaign. The difference between the two comes down to intention and usage. A slogan can reveal itself as a tagline, and a tagline can be used as an advertising slogan.

One of the most-admired taglines, Nike's "Just do it," began as an advertising slogan in 1988. Its author Dan Wieden, founder of the Wieden + Kennedy agency, was inspired by the last words of convicted murderer Gary Gilmore before his execution, "Let's do it"—incidentally affirming that inspiration can come from anywhere.

The campaign was wildly successful. "Just do it" became a call for everyone, regardless of ability, to participate in some form of physical activity. As Nike defines it, "If you have a body, you are an athlete." Therefore, the phrase applies to both internal and external audiences and aligns with the company's mission of bringing "inspiration and innovation to every athlete in the world."

"Just do it" then informs the filtering criteria when designing product packaging (easy to open, clearly labeled), websites (easy to navigate, quick to load), or products themselves (sturdy, easy to put on, does not constrict free movement).

Another ideal combination tagline/slogan is the Ritz-Carlton Hotel Company's "We are ladies and gentlemen serving ladies and gentlemen." While setting expectations for customer service and mutual respect between coworkers, it also empowers employees to take additional measures to ensure customer satisfaction.

These are ideal situations where a phrase aligns with brand values. Regrettably the ideal is overwhelmed by the glib and clever. Now there is nothing inherently wrong with cleverness, but when it is a self-satisfied cleverness, the resulting line distances the reader.

A recent campaign for Marcus, Goldman Sachs's first foray into consumer banking, used the line "you can money." There is no stated promise of capabilities, access, or results, just attitude. And in the case of Goldman Sachs, an attitude that too-perfectly conforms to the general public perception of an arrogant, exploitative large investment bank. Here, a line that could have been a magical incantation, ends up summoning a demon.

Nike's "Just do it," began as an advertising slogan and eventually became a call for everyone, regardless of ability, to be physically active.

Branding is about how we live with branded objects not how we buy them.

A brand's intimate relationship to its customers must remain under continual adjustment. The analysis of user interactions were previously informed by comparing medians and averages with the direct observation of people by urbanists, sociologists, and other disciplines. Conclusions and updated standards were then extrapolated from relatively small data sets and acted upon by relatively small teams.

Today computer technology allows for massively large amounts of data to be distilled into sharp insights with little delay. And that information is now acted upon by a seemingly infinite number of algorithms and bots, with one manifestation being customer relationship management software or CRM. Such platforms track customer interactions and sales, organize and prioritize opportunities, and enable interaction between divisions.

In his later work, German philosopher Martin Heidegger distinguished between calculative thinking and meditative thinking. Calculative thinking proposes ideas, plans goals, and is basically tactical and future-facing. Meditative thinking, on the other hand, is a "letting-dwell" that reflects on reality and allows for a certain clarity about the situation of life and being.

The dazzling, technological wonders of the digital order reward calculative brand thinking. But they also rob producers and consumers of the ability to reflect upon their relationship to the brand and to each other. In such a condition, every interaction is an opportunity for a sale. There is no intimacy between audience and brand. The message is "buy me."

A humorous tweet from American brand strategist Russ Meyer puts it well: "CRM is why I'm getting birthday greetings from companies I haven't frequented in years. Thanks??"

Perhaps the reason branding is seen with so much cynicism is that "buy me" is often the default. Once one purchases a new bed, how necessary are follow-up emails promoting a new bed, which is the exact same bed? The bed is already home and part of the owner's life. It's difficult to have a deeper relationship with a bed than sleeping in it.

Meditative brand thinking, on the other hand, suspends the immediately actionable in favor of the propositional. It is comfortable maintaining a "what if?" It considers the realities of how a brand lives with its audience and vice versa. Meditative brand thinking dwells in the senses: the brand as an experience instead of an abstract concept, the brand as something that dwells with its consumer, the brand as a kind of family member.

The message of meditative brand thinking, of brand thinking that lets dwell, then becomes "take me home." And it's difficult to think of a sentence more intimate than "take me home."

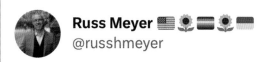

Russ Meyer 🇺🇸 🌻 ▬ 🌻 ▬
@russhmeyer

CRM is why I'm getting birthday greetings from companies I haven't frequented in years.
Thanks??

6:42 PM • Jan 29, 2022

This tweet by American brand strategist Russ Meyer captures the false sense of intimacy generated by customer relationship management software.

Pop-up shops are
potential media events.

A pop-up shop, or a temporary retail venue, can be an ideal way to test out or introduce new products, a brand extension, or a cobranded partnership. The ephemerality of the venture helps create a bit of drama, and, if done well, there can be a halo effect as well.

And, depending on the brand, it doesn't even have to be a shop. An art exhibit or short musical series built around the brand might underscore cultural relevance or vitality. PornHub's brief 2017 pop-up shop in SoHo was open for only a month and mainly sold branded apparel, but it did draw major media attention and helped reveal the wide appeal of a brand that wasn't widely spoken about.

In the past, pop-ups were best opened where influential news and publishing channels were headquartered. Having a concentrated audience of editors, writers, and producers—media gatekeepers, continually on the lookout for content—maximized the allocated budget and energy expended. This usually meant urban centers like New York City, Los Angeles, or London. But with print and broadcast media's gradual loss of market share, and the rise of the digital realm, locations that reflect more specific demo- and psychographic profiles came to the forefront. This was Brooklyn, Shoreditch, or Oberkampf: hip neighborhoods teeming with influencers and other social gatekeepers who can do a lot of heavy cognitive lifting for a pop-up.

But even those neighborhoods will reach a semiotic saturation where they will no longer mean as much as they used to. And as people leave once-hip neighborhoods due to COVID or rising prices, newer, cooler ones will take their place.

The task of deciding where to locate pop-ups, or whether the effort would be better expended in another form, is becoming more difficult for brands. Social media influence is hard to predict, so any alignment with a cool neighborhood can quickly be seen as inauthentic—a menu selection rather than a genuine alignment.

The cult beauty brand Summer Fridays teamed with Upside Pizza
in New York's SoHo for a pop-up, featuring food and limited-edition
apparel in March 2023.

Brand colors influence
brand associations.

When one thinks of the American luxury jeweler Tiffany & Co., the distinctive robin-egg blue of the packaging immediately comes to mind. It is so culturally attached that one doesn't even have to see the logo to know that what is inside lives up to the company standards of materials, craftsmanship, and quality.

Tiffany Blue, in and of itself, does not mean anything. But since its first appearance on a company catalog in 1845, it has come to be associated with Tiffany's values and products. It "means" Tiffany only because of its consistent usage. It means Tiffany only in context. Seeing an egg that color in a nest would make most people think "robin," not "Tiffany."

Why is it that when people present color palettes, they justify their choices by ascribing psychological or symbolic attributes? These attributes are rooted only by cultural association, over time, and have no inherent meaning in themselves. Black may be the color of death in the West, but in Asia death is signified by white. To insist on one-to-one correlations between colors and a meaning isn't taking historical or cultural antecedents into account.

For example, the red soles of Christian Louboutin shoes have historical precedent in Louis XIV, who ruled that only those in royal favor were allowed to have red heels on their shoes. Red heels became a way to track the workings and hierarchies of the court. Now they signal the workings and hierarchies of the well-to-do. The specific meaning may have changed, but the use is similar.

Another consideration of color is its phenomenological nature. Emergency vehicles use red and blue lights because each color appears at different ends of the visible spectrum: red has the longest wavelength and blue the shortest. This ensures that the combination will be visible to people with different degrees of colorblindness.

There is also energy in combinations of color. Complementary colors at the same value tend to vibrate visually. This is an instance where color doesn't respond to the question of, "What does it mean?" But it becomes a matter of, "What does it do?" This expands a color palette into a palette of actions, easier to equate to brand behavior than a symbolic one—transforming the visual rainbow into a full spectrum.

And over time, the gestural, phenomenological, or historical use of color is where the symbolic associations are reinforced.

Red soles on a pair of Christian Louboutin shoes.

Well-intentioned stress testing within branding teams leads to better results.

A fallacy familiar to anyone planning a branding project is imagining an ideal, frictionless process. In such a scenario, the strategy side begins with customer segmentation and research, devises a strategic plan, which is approved by the client, and submits it to creative for realization. The creative work is then presented to strategy for approval, adjustments are made, and then everything is submitted to the client.

In reality a whole buffet of human emotions, misunderstandings, and contrary intentions frequently appear, turning into bitterness, resentment, and acrimony. This may be a result of how the work is framed. And since branding is such a varied process, it seems appropriate to address how disciplines interact and hopefully to identify a useful approach in managing this diversity.

The geodesic dome serves as an ideal model when speaking about teams and other organizational issues. Invented by German engineer Walther Bauersfeld in 1925, it was popularized after the Second World War by American architect and systems theorist Buckminster Fuller during his tenure at Black Mountain College.

The structural principle that keeps the dome up is known as tensile integrity, which Fuller combined into "tensegrity." This is a system that avoids applying shear stresses or bending forces upon its elements. Nothing is twisted or torqued. Once everything is in place, the mutual and distributed pressure upon all elements strengthens the overall structure, which can then efficiently cover wide areas without the need for columns.

Mutual pressure and tension define the ideal relationship between the two main brand building activities of strategy and design. It is best if all involved are detached from their ego—which is easier said than done—and that individual tastes are focused toward the benefit of the project. In this environment, comments like, "I think blue is too close to our competition's color palette," are better than an insistent, "I just don't like blue." All comments and suggestions have to be qualifiable.

Eventually, if mutual best intentions are acknowledged—where all questions, mistranslations, and unexpected interpretations are directed toward the sake of the project—within an honest and open environment, the work becomes better.

From the start, this tensegrity of disciplines should be explicitly defined and cultivated across the organization. Nothing great is ever easy. Disagreements can be gifts. Objections show that an idea is being considered. And being asked to explain oneself strengthens the idea. Throughout this discourse, the opportunity to learn from other disciplines is constantly present, trust is earned, and the work is directed toward the benefit of the audience.

The mutual and distributed pressure upon all elements of a geodesic dome strengthens the overall structure, which can then efficiently cover wide areas without the need for columns.

Language should be used purposefully, not decoratively.

In a written correspondence with Slovenian philosopher Slavoj Žižek, the Canadian sociologist Duane Rousselle points out the strangeness of what he calls "word art." Word art appears as bits of inspirational and motivational language written large on a wall, on a mass-produced pillow, or in your Instagram feed. WeWork locations famously had "Love what you do" across walls, staff T-shirts, and elevator screens. Some Starbucks locations feature neon sculpture that reads "Coffee = togetherness." And there are hundreds of iterations of "Live, love, laugh" available in any number of big-box houseware stores.

Word art as a form had early origins in conceptual art of the 1960s. Joseph Kosuth and Lawrence Weiner were the first to work in the realm of "art as idea," where the easiest way of conveying that idea was through language. Kosuth would display photostats of dictionary definitions or phrases made in neon, and Weiner painted text in his personal typeface on the gallery wall. More recently, the English artist Tracey Emin's handwritten, confessional texts enlarged into neon installations have become popular highlights in museums around the world—and in visitor's Instagram feeds.

It might seem logical for brands to consider displaying their tag lines, values or mottos in an equally elevated manner. It establishes an environment and is another way to influence the customer experience. And as Rousselle suggests, it may also be intended to create a nontransactional atmosphere—a "retreat from the madness of capitalist hyper-activity." But Žižek points out that such text is "wisdom instead of proper thinking." The audience is fascinated by something that at first glance sounds deep but is more like intellectual comfort food.

These platitudes are bits of nonthinking. Thinking is open-ended, allowing for varieties of expression, multiple methods, and diverging conclusions. To create a space where one's audience is encouraged to think for themselves is to consider the brand's erotic potential.

Besides the intellectual suppression of the audience, word-art wisdom is in danger of becoming another box to check on the brand-building checklist. It is currently quite common for brand presentations to include environmental applications where the founder's signature is scrawled across a wall, a poster displays the brand's values, or an on-brand inspirational phrase sits by the main entrance. All of these can be an opportunity to encourage true, deep, reflective thinking. But in order to achieve that, an equally deep bit of reflective thinking needs to be done.

Note:
See 34. Erotics of Brands.

Platitudes writ large, like this neon sign that reads "Make it Happen,"
are moments of nonthinking.

90 TIME

Brands need to honor and respect the role of time.

The structure of a recipe is very simple: a list of ingredients and a step-by-step process. Both seem to be self-explanatory. But upon reflection, this broad division tends to constrain crucial elements into process, when it might be helpful to view them as ingredients in themselves. For example, whether thawing, fermenting, proofing, or cooking, time is more than just a procedural step; it is truly a transformative ingredient. One has to add time in the correct proportions, like flour, salt, or anything else.

Time as ingredient is a potential metaphor for the creative process. Instead of marginalizing it to something meted out to maintain efficiency or, worse, the enemy of production schedules, time allows for deep observation and reflection. Alternatives to rushed responses—which may be logical but superficial—could be anything from a better reframing of the situation to the creation of a wholly different market.

Our accelerated society puts ever-increasing demands on our attention and cognitive ability. The Italian philosopher Franco "Bifo" Berardi describes one condition of this pressure as semio-inflation: "When you need more signs, words, and information to buy less meaning."

In 1986, after a demonstration at a proposed McDonald's location at the foot of the Spanish Steps in Rome, a group of activists founded the Slow Food movement. Their manifesto claimed that "under the sign of Industrialization, this century first invented the machine and then modeled its lifestyle after it. Speed became our shackles. We fell prey to the same virus: 'the fast life'… fractures our customs and assails us even in our own homes…"

On a parallel line, Carolyn F. Strauss and Alastair Fuad-Luke's Slow Design movement advocates for the deceleration of resource consumption and production. Both groups see society's focus on ever-increasing productivity as contributing to environmental and cultural decline.

Therefore, slow creativity—let's call it Slow Branding—might help shift the development and distribution of brands away from the sole domain of the producer's needs toward the mutual health and success of producer, audience, and environment.

One of the great gifts each of us has been given is time. And attending to its passage deeply reveals life's texture, especially as seasons and holidays come around again and again. We have associations about time that are brandlike. These associations place us in culture and history, and they gather us into close affiliations.

Our modern commercial society has trashed this world and is rapidly eating what is left. Our social body has lost touch with the poetic, the dreamt, and the natural, all for the sake of increased production and profit—and at the expense of time.

The Slow Food Condotta Valle Ossola agricultural education project
near Domodossola, Italy.

One of the basic building blocks of branding is the touchpoint.

Branding professionals within the English-speaking world have a particular word that describes every opportunity for a brand to enter someone's consciousness. That word is touchpoint.

Traditionally the definition was limited to describe discrete points of interaction: a brochure, a package, speaking with a salesperson, an identity system, a store. But if brands are associations held in the mind, then this doesn't seem to adequately represent the complex hypermessaged world we live in. Touchpoints are more than the transactional moments of purchasing, delivering, and opening. They also comprise the liminal moments of awareness when learning about a brand, hearing about it in passing, or seeing a logo out of the corner of your eye.

Watching a friend open an app on a smartphone is a touchpoint. As is trying on a pair of shoes, seeing a roadside sign for a restaurant, or arranging to meet someone in front of a shop.

Even legends can be a touchpoint. There is a story, which still occasionally appears in news media, of a customer returning tires to Nordstrom—a retailer which has never sold tires. In 1975 Nordstrom acquired three Alaskan stores from a company that did sell tires. When the legendary customer brought back the tires to the same building in which they were purchased—a building with a new logo on the exterior and different products on display—the return was approved.

M&Ms candies have also acquired customer-developed attributes that have nothing to do with the brand but are, in effect, brand touchpoints. During the 1970s, stories of the aphrodisiac powers of green-colored candies began to circulate, followed by the tale of rock band Van Halen's tour contract, which demanded a bowl of M&Ms with all the brown ones removed. These, too, are touchpoints.

Brand touchpoints can have a crucial role in the valuation of a company. Consider, for instance, a financial services company. The basic value of their products is easily counted. One just has to look at the profitability of their various offerings. But how does one determine the value of the company's brand?

Even if one applies a small amount of value to every liminal, casual perceptive moment of any trace of a brand's presence, one quickly sees the cumulative value of brand touchpoints—and the effect of brand on a company's overall value.

As the potential for touchpoints to burnish or diminish is understood, one begins to grasp the almost maddening, and virtually impossible task of managing a brand. It is many times more difficult than picking out all the brown candies in a bowl of M&Ms.

Even a brief reflection of a T-Mobile logo glimpsed in the window of a Reebok store counts as a touchpoint.

A brand's impact on the overall value of the company is commonly accepted. Why wouldn't it be? If the price someone is willing to pay for something is driven by an abstract perception like value, then it seems to be logical and true.

Problem is, the relationship is impossible to measure objectively. Anyone who attempts to rank brand value—and there are many who do—tends to have an interest in the matter. Brand value comes into play when a company is purchased or goes public and when the internal brand team or external agency needs to justify their activity.

There is no Archimedean point from which we might properly survey brand values. It may be a messy, squishy business, but it is a necessary task if one is going to speak to the power of brand within an organization.

A relatively simple but admittedly tedious method is to begin by collecting the appearance of a logo on all brand touchpoints and assigning them a modest, singular value. For example, if this is done for an international bank, that list would include logos on all signage, webpages, digital banner ads, credit cards (both issued by the bank and cobranded), bank statements, advertisements for the brand, cobranded advertisements where the logo appears amongst other logos, promotional materials, stationery, coffee mugs, pens, tie clips, tote bags, ATM receipts, the ATMs that spit out the receipts—and so on. Digital versions would be tracked by user data, the analog by units produced. The goal is to count all appearances not engagements. A peripheral appearance, flashing by on a bus ad or along the side of a webpage, counts.

If one then values each appearance modestly—say, 50 cents to a dollar—the total for such a brand would still be in the millions, if not billions, of dollars.

This method accounts for touchpoints that are classified as "paid" (advertising, placement, etc.) and "owned" (produced by the brand) accounting for "earned" touchpoints (editorial mentions, social media posts, etc.) may be close to impossible but would add to the total amount.

Global consumer brands that sell merchandise would have an even higher valuation. Imagine the cumulative perceptual effect of all the T-shirts sporting Mickey Mouse, the Coca-Cola logo, or Tickle Me Elmo; across all possible contexts from playgrounds, to city sidewalks, to mug shots.[1] All appearances, free and loose of any other situating criteria, have the potential to introduce someone who may not know about the brand—regardless where the touchpoint was intended to appear along the customer journey. That, in itself, has some financial impact on a brand's value.

Note:
1. The Smoking Gun website has a growing collection of police mug shots that feature some perpetrators wearing Sesame Street character T-shirts.

Actor Wilmer Valderrama in a Mickey Mouse T-shirt at the
The Dukes of Hazzard premiere, in Grauman's Chinese Theatre,
Los Angeles, CA, on July 28, 2005.

93 VALUES

All aspects of a brand should connect back to its purpose.

In describing a product—let's say a hammer—one can describe its shape, size, weight, and the materials that went into its manufacture. Additionally one can describe the context where a hammer is commonly found. All of these qualities, while accurate, are incomplete unless we know what the hammer is used for—in this case, to strike another object so the hand is not harmed.

When it comes to people, there are many, often competing, theories about what our purpose is. It could be reproduction, the acquisition of knowledge, or just simple pleasure. Regardless of the definition, each purpose needs a support structure for it to be reached. In the case of the hammer, it needs something to strike and someone to do the striking.

The world is full of objects. And once we see something at hand as useful, we elevate it into something with a purpose. In other words, we assign meaning and purpose to the things around us in order to make sense of the universe.

One of the standard procedures in brand development is to establish a set of values for which the brand stands. These are (should be) an expression of the brand's purpose and can be projected into any length of time. For example, the dating app Hinge's stated goal is to be deleted. If they are successful, their users won't need the app anymore. Besides their employees and users, Hinge's purposed support structure includes a set of principles: designed for deletion, radical trust, embracing failure, adhering to their principles (very meta), and only working with people who have heart. These values are the ethical and political foundation for decisions made at Hinge, made in the hope that their users will no longer need them.

When writing brand values, it can be difficult to maintain clarity. This is because there is no one, agreed-upon format. One brand can have a single set of values while another will have a set of principles, each built upon values, all laddered up into a "North Star" purpose, and requiring Talmudic exegesis in order to guide a UX designer who just wants to design a navigation bar.

This most likely reflects rounds of client meetings, where a multitude of voices sound off in a setting without a final arbiter. One suspects that the duplications in Hinge's principles are the result of just such a setting. For clarity, consider defining future brand values simply, with an end goal and a support system in place; one designed to clear the space needed in order to reach that end.

The values and goals of a hammer's potential use determine its final form.

Pay attention to what the
audience wants a brand
to be.

When brands are fully integrated into the market, fusing with popular culture, each may be influenced by the other. And if a brand is paying attention, its presence in everyday language may signal opportunities for expansion into new territories and markets.

In 1980 the Sugarhill Gang released "Rapper's Delight," an early hip-hop single featuring three rappers boasting of their fame and fortune—their cars, financial accounts, sexual exploits, the clothes in their closets—which established the standard hip-hop narrative. Within that context, hip-hop expressed an aspirational relationship with luxury brands (Gucci, Fendi, Louis Vuitton, etc.) which, at that time, had little interest in audiences outside their tightly focused target audience.

Brands signal all sorts of things: our current place in society and where we would like to be. And hip-hop culture saw the language of luxury brands as both a means for rebellion and transcendence. But there was a disconnect. Brands like Gucci didn't necessarily produce products with the sizes, silhouettes, styling, or details that the hip-hop audience required; nor were they easily accessible.

The hip-hop audience bridged this gap through the work of couturier Daniel Day, aka Dapper Dan. Opening in 1982, Day's Harlem boutique quickly became a favorite stop for rappers, gangsters, and boxers, serving clients twenty-four hours a day, seven days a week.

Day developed a method of silk-screening onto soft leather and used it to print patterns of appropriated logos, sometimes mixing different ones on the same garment. And as his clientele increasingly appeared in media and on album packages, he drew the attention of trademark lawyers. After years of raids and lawsuits, Day closed shop in 1992.

Day continued to service a select clientele but at a much smaller scale. And the occasional celebrity would appear on a red carpet wearing Dapper Dan. In 1999 Lil' Kim appeared on the cover of *Interview* magazine with a Louis Vuitton logo pattern on her skin. And a 2008 Britany Spears music video featured a pink Hummer with a Louis Vuitton pattern across the dashboard. Culturally Dapper Dan never went away.

At a 2017 fashion show, Alessandro Michele, Gucci's creative director, presented a jacket resembling a 1989 Dapper Dan model. After fielding criticisms of cultural appropriation, Gucci declared it an "homage." Several months later Day opened an appointment-only studio for custom clients, "powered" by Gucci, which supplied the raw materials.

And in an example of a brand learning from a previously ignored (if not adversarial) market, the partnership later released a ready-to-wear and accessories collection, which took a "cue from the Dapper Dan archive" but was "created with the House's refined materials." The copier was now the copied—and an equal partner.

A U.K. Gucci advertisement featuring Daniel Day, known as
Dapper Dan.

The way branding professionals speak colors how they see their audience.

There are two renaissance traditions that have given us the modern branding professional: the atelier, originating in the workshops of artisans, and the office, which evolved in governments and trading companies. And the echoes of those two traditions resonate in the language of branding.

The atelier was where the eye was sharpened, individual touch was refined, and one's taste was developed. Regardless of medium, its apprenticeship system established a baseline of craft upon which subsequent generations could innovate. Each new step was, in a way, a dialogue with the past, built on tradition and with a sense of lineage.

Even though history has eroded the apprenticeship/master tradition, there is still a family tree quality to today's studios. The personalities and details of a person's previous experience places them in that culture.

The office tradition is another thing entirely. Built around the mind, it sees the world as a collection of reserves and resources. The goals are acquisition, growth, and profit. While there may be a bit of the apprenticeship system in the office, the methods can be taught differently because they are intellectual and analytical.

This allows for a different kind of expression, one that objectifies the material and people involved in the office. A certain kind of alienation is at hand and, as a result, language shifts.

The governmental and institutional origins of the office lead to a militaristic tone, a tone that is pervasive in modern branding. Audiences are seen as targets, the focus of campaigns. The goal is to win accounts, acquire territories, and defeat the competition.

"How did the presentation go?"

"We killed it."

"Good thing we made the deck in the war room."

But the language of the atelier, the studio, is much different. It is the language of relationships. One speaks of alignment, centering, and proportion. Objects are in relation to each other.

Branding is concerned with how people feel. It seems appropriate for practitioners to be as thoughtful as possible. To see their audience with empathy rather than as a means towards an abstract, short-term goal, like growth or profit.

Working for the short-term goal is not the same as building a relationship over time. That requires a different mindset, beginning with what one calls their audience.

There are numerous traditions and authors, spiritual and secular, who see the divine in others. For example, Ralph Waldo Emerson called it the "god-within." While a branding practitioner need not go to that extreme, such a way of thinking and speaking does help set a course for an empathic approach to one's audience. Because words are the first expression of thoughts.

Top: The atelier, where traditions, materials, and processes are united.
Bottom: The office, which sees the world as a collection of reserves and resources.

Every brand has a
vulnerability.

Deadheading is the practice of carrying airline staff on a normal passenger trip to properly locate them for an upcoming shift. In 2017 four deadheading employees were assigned to board United Express Flight 3411 departing from Chicago O'Hare International Airport. The flight was fully booked and in order to make room for the deadheaders, employees offered travel vouchers to any passenger willing to vacate their seats. None of the paying passengers accepted.

Employees then had to select four paying customers to be involuntarily deplaned. According to passenger accounts, an airline supervisor stepped onto the plane and "brusquely announced, 'We have United employees that need to fly to Louisville tonight. ... This flight's not leaving until four people get off.'"[1] With no volunteers, a manager boarded and informed the passengers that four of them would be chosen by computer.

Three of the four agreed to leave. The fourth, pulmonologist Dr. David Dao Duy Anh, politely refused to deplane, calmly explaining that he needed to see patients the following day. Chicago Department of Aviation Security officers were then called to remove him. In the process, Dao's face struck an armrest, apparently knocking him unconscious. The officers then dragged him by his arms past rows of onlooking passengers, some recording the incident with their camera phones.

Once smartphone footage and reports of the incident hit social media, there was wide, public outroar. Two of the security officers were dismissed and the remaining suspended; the Chicago Department of Aviation's security office was decertified; stock prices in United's holding company fell; and consumer preference polls showed that flyers would be willing to spend more money not to fly United.

In one badly executed event; five decades of United Airlines' "Fly the Friendly Skies" brand campaign, introduced in 1965, was rendered worthless.

It is easy to direct blame at the individuals involved. They may not have been properly trained; but they were also encouraged to view passengers as numbers and not as people. The deadheading employees had to take that flight because United had stretched service routes to impossibly thin coverage. Airport employees were probably working toward, and measured against, increasingly tighter performance metrics. And airlines, in general, operate in a difficult regulatory and financial environment.

In each case, the benchmark was profit and not people. We talk about how brands concern themselves with personal relationships, but until we find a way to track individual compensation with metrics other than efficiency and profitability that mindset will remain every brand's weakest link.

Note:
1. Caryn Rousseau And David Koenig, "United has police literally drag a passenger off an overbooked plane to make room for employees," April 10, 2017, *The Salt Lake Tribune*.

When brand benchmarks focus on profit and not people, the results
can resemble this 2021 protest during the UN Climate Change
Conference in Glasgow, Scotland.

Can a brand simply be a way to spend time?

In the book *In Praise of Good Bookstores*, Jeff Deutsch notes, "The good bookstore sells books, but its primary product, if you will, is the browsing experience."[1] This wonderfully captures the laddering effect of a brand and how brands overlap and create a halo effect.

This is easily graspable when thinking about lifestyle brands like Ralph Lauren or Marie Kondo. Both accommodate variations of style—from industrial/modern to spiritual/minimal—yet still convey a distinctive character. Ralph Lauren's brand—whether it be distressed jeans, velvet suits, house paint, or sportswear—grounds its customers within a vague historical lineage, which then burnishes how they see themselves. And Marie Kondo, whether it be desk/kitchen/closet organizers, garden tools, or decorative objects, gives her customers an accessible and stylistic control over their daily life.

More targeted brands may have a smaller catalog, but they too can contribute to a similar cumulative effect. Playing a recording from the legendary jazz label Blue Note in a small bar in Tokyo's Shinjuku Golden Gai district or in a high-end audiophile shop adds a sophistication to the moment. But the Golden Gai bar's product is a certain worldliness, while the audiophile shop is still audio equipment. The difference is that in Golden Gai, the recording is used as a signifier, and in the audiophile shop the recording is merely an evaluation tool.

What then is the difference between the two? Perhaps it is the usage of time itself. The bar, and bookstore, both encourage repeat visits and lingering. The customer can align their sensibilities with anyone else there, building a small sense of community. Anything for sale, regardless of where it came from, collectively defines that experience.

This describes why bookstores, and now Ralph Lauren shops, have cafés. They are selling a way to use time itself. Which is a fascinating aspect of branding: the manner in how one spends time is a brand.

The opportunities to gather and define other phenomena into a brand are almost infinite. The way one raises their children can be a brand. Or the way one walks, sleeps, breathes, etc. can be a brand. All are potential locations where products can gather to define that particular space. To the layman, it may sound ridiculous, but it can also be a way to redirect how people consume into something more mindful and considered.

Note:
1, Jeff Deutsch. *In Praise of Good Bookstores*, 2022, Princeton University Press, Princeton, NJ.

The Ralph Lauren flagship store in New York's Upper East Side now has
a café; where customers can spend time in a Ralph Lauren manner.

Brands can define
complete ways of being.

The term "lifestyle brand" is certainly well-known enough. When a product, or collection of products, represents a group mindset so efficiently, it has reached the exalted level of lifestyle brand.

Martha Stewart is a classic example. There is a Martha Stewart way to bake a cake, a Martha Stewart way to mix a cocktail, a Martha Stewart way to decorate a home, a Martha Stewart way to dress, and a Martha Stewart way to enjoy that cake and cocktail, in that home, while wearing those clothes.

This perfectly describes the far-reaching potential of branding. There are no limits to what can be absorbed into the brand, no disciplinary boundaries, no categories to observe. With just a small bit of imagination, one could define a Martha Stewart way to enter the metaverse or a Martha Stewart way to travel between planets.

"Lifestyle brand" is not a new, or unique, concept. The term *Gesamtkunstwerk*, identified by the German Romantics and best associated with the composer Richard Wagner, translates to "total work of art" and is probably the best example of a desire to connect diverse forms under one mindset. It is an ambitious goal that could describe diverse forms, including the output of British designer and activist William Morris, instructors and students of the Bauhaus, architect Frank Lloyd Wright, or German designer Dieter Rams.

Like today's lifestyle brands, these attempts to create the *Gesamtkunstwerk*, proposed alternate ways to live. And because of their hypothetical nature, each is, to some degree, utopian.

There is a tension in every utopia, between the included and the excluded. The *Gesamtkunstwerks* of Morris, the Bauhaus, Wright, Rams, and Martha Stewart each carry a material cost of admission. Sometimes it's as incidental as a tea cup; sometimes it's a house on a plot of land. But the modern brand can admit members without these restrictions.

If there are no limits to what can make up a brand, then could something so insignificant as a hashtag be a brand? In the case of #blacklivesmatter, the answer is definitely "yes."

#blacklivesmatter groups like-minded people under a shared vision of the world they would like to live in. It is utopian and world-building, just like any other lifestyle brand. And it efficiently describes an individual with as much precision as Martha Stewart or any other lifestyle brand.

In fact, #blacklivesmatter has had more cultural effect than many other lifestyle brands. It has transformed governmental and institutional policies, shifted the cultural conversation, is used on both sides of political debates, and appears on T-shirts. Perhaps it could be argued that #blacklivesmatter is the first total lifestyle brand.

The Black Lives Matter brand grew beyond its American origins into a global phenomenon, as shown in this June 2020 image from a demonstration in London.

There's a distinct difference between brands and personalities.

"Brand" has become so ubiquitous so as to be meaningless. Therefore, as an attempt to maintain a degree of precision, let us distinguish between "brand" and "personality."

We all have "that friend." The one who sticks out in some way: always running late, loves manga, or wears all black. And when speaking about them in a certain situation, we might say they were either "on brand" or "off brand." And some of us might know a person claiming to be "working on my brand," when in reality they are going to school, making TikToks, or updating their resumé.

These two examples show how the word "brand" has detached from its marketing origins and is now floating freely in everyday usage.

Brands have a metonymic relationship with products, organizations, collectively held beliefs, or any form of cultural/political grouping. Metonymic because they establish connections in the mind: avocado toast connects to the lifestyles of young, urban professionals; Range Rovers connect to privilege; and Walmart connects to rural America. By eating avocado toast, driving Range Rovers, or spending our Saturdays at Walmart, we place ourselves within their respective cultural spheres and find our place in the world.

Like individuals, brands have personalities. And those personalities help distinguish the associations held in people's minds.

Individuals become brands when their associations involve a call to an action that involves more than a handful of people. Barack Obama connects with a progressive social agenda. And when he speaks about a topic, we're moved to action because of the emotions we ascribe to him, not by his logical argument nor his personality. We are either inspired to vote in line with his agenda or for candidates or referendums that are in opposition.

This suggests that brands are less specific, yet more evocative, than personalities. And that may be the source of their power.

Isaac Mizrahi doesn't have a well-defined brand—he produced garments for his own line and others, designed Broadway costumes, appears on television, and has a cabaret act—but he has a very distinct personality that is constantly displayed on social media.

Ralph Lauren, on the other hand, has a very well-defined brand that has grown beyond clothing into housewares, furniture, and paint. We can look at several different chairs, for example, and immediately identify the one which is more "Ralph Lauren." But few of us could describe his personality beyond a vague affinity with the American West and vintage cars. Ultimately what made Ralph Lauren a billionaire wasn't his personality; it was his ability to convey the feeling of his brand without having to say a word.

Barack Obama's association with cultural and political groupings evoked different brand-level responses.
Top: An Obama rally held the day before the 2012 election in Madison, Wisconsin.
Bottom: An anti-G20 protest on November 15, 2014, in Brisbane, Australia.

The aesthetics of our interaction and consumption of brands tend to fall within three general categories.

Since brands are "consumed" in some manner—they are either eaten, used, subscribed to, or followed—some attention should be paid to the aesthetics of modern brand consumption.

American cultural theorist and scholar Sianne Ngai in her 2012 book *Our Aesthetic Categories*[1], argued that the categories best-suited to reflect today's hyper-commodified, performance-driven, late-capitalist society were the zany, cute, and informative. They correspond with how we produce, consume, and choose today.

The zany resonates with the precariousness of modern work. Like the episode of *I Love Lucy* where a chocolate-wrapping line is impossibly sped up, the modern workplace demands more productivity with fewer resources. Workers do more for less money, under increased oversight, and with less personal time during a shift. Any Amazon warehouse employee can attest to this.

The cute describes the power relationship between consumer and the consumed. The cute is powerless and in need of our protection or cultivation. We bring it into the home. But the cute extends beyond the usual models of Hello Kitty, Sailor Moon, or *E.T.* It can also, counterintuitively, be a way to process the horrifying. The Freddie Kruegers of our imagination are eventually defeated and lose their power—which may explain sexy *Nightmare on Elm Street* Halloween costumes. Rendering something as cute, then, is how we empower ourselves when facing the world.

The informative is our space of judgment. We scroll through reviews, watch Instagram Reels, and measure our consumption patterns against current trends. Upon learning about the detrimental effects of single-use plastic, we collectively stop using plastic straws. But we still prefer that our salad greens arrive in plastic bags. The informative isn't a fully comprehensive space but is just informative enough to allow us to maintain existing patterns. We prefer to appear informed, but we end up making emotional decisions.

There are many roads that lead to the creation of a brand. But the current state of media, the poverty of today's public discourse, and cultural inertia have limited how we aesthetically engage with the marketplace. Since aesthetics trigger emotions, this helps explain the limited palette of our expressive spectrum.

The call for all of us, creators and consumers alike, is to approach each other and the objects of the world as thoughtfully as possible. And to try and rediscover the magic contained within the smallest moments of interaction between each.

Note:
1. Sianne Ngai. *Our Aesthetic Categories*. 2012. Harvard University Press. Cambridge, Massachusetts and London, England.

Two examples that conform to Sianne Ngai's description of empowerment through "cute."
Left: A sexy *Nightmare on Elm Street* Halloween costume.
Right: Hello Kitty band-aids.

ABOUT THE AUTHOR

Mark Kingsley is a creative director and strategist with a wide range of experience and recognition. As Executive Strategy Director at Collins, he developed the new global positioning for Ogilvy and helped Equinox enter the luxury hotel business. At Landor, Mark was the global creative lead on the Citi account—overseeing everything from design, intranet development, workshops, and global brand audits. Additionally he was part of Ogilvy's Brand Innovation Group (BIG), created Hewlett-Packard advertising for Publicis & Hal Riney, and designed fragrance packaging at Cosmair.

For over 17 years, his studio Greenberg Kingsley specialized in music and arts, creating several years of branding and advertising for Central Park SummerStage; products for the Guggenheim Museum store; and music packaging for Blue Note Records, John Coltrane, Pat Metheny, Quincy Jones, Ginger Baker, Jewel, and Yes. During this time, his work received a Grammy nomination, and was selected for AIGA 50 Books/50 Covers.

Mark speaks and writes about design and branding, and is on the faculty at the School of Visual Arts Masters in Branding program, where he teaches a class in the application of critical theory to brand strategy. That approach to brand strategy fuels the work of his current studio, Malcontent (malcontent.com). His current client list includes global brand agencies, feature film directors, and fashion startups.

In 2016 he was profiled in *Print* magazine as one of "56 Inspiring Designers Shaping Our World Today." And he was a subject of professor Alice Twemlow's PhD thesis, published in 2017 by MIT Press as *Sifting the Trash: A History of Design Criticism*.

ACKNOWLEDGMENTS

A thinking life begins with influential teachers. Mine include Robert C. Morgan, R. Roger Remington, Ajay Singh Chaudhary, and Mihai Nadin.

An experienced life requires colleagues and clients. My global network at Landor, friends in various agencies and studios, and my art world/music industry clients opened many doors, opportunities, and perspectives.

Ideas need a place to live. My eternal gratitude to Debbie Millman for building the Masters in Branding program at the School of Visual Arts in New York City, and for clearing a space for me to grow. My fellow faculty and students graced me with inspiration, encouragement, opposing ideas, and suggestions worth pursuing.

Writers need readers. Thank you to Dr. Tom Guarriello, Melinda Welch, Kristin James, Kelsy Postlethwait, Michael Shirey, Mikel Rouse, and Jane Brown for their feedback and encouragement. And my deepest thanks to this book's de facto dramaturge, Lisa Sheridan, who read everything, workshopped half-baked ideas, and helped bang everything into a proper shape.

Books need publishers. Thank you to my editor Jonathan Simcosky for his eternal patience and encouragement, and thank you to the staff at Quarto/Rockport for their additional patience and energy.

I have been blessed with caring and supportive family members and friends—some long passed, some recent additions. This book is a testament to your love.

INDEX